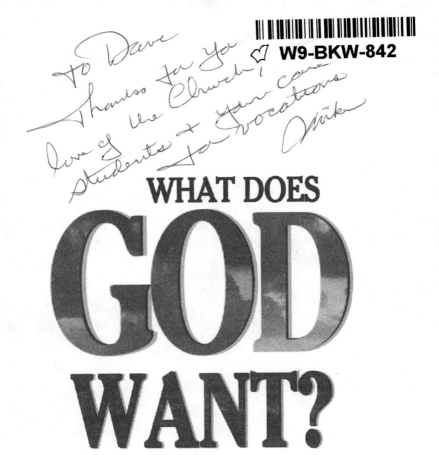

To Dave
Thanks for yo
love of the Church!
Students + your care
for Vocations
Mike

WHAT DOES

GOD

WANT?

Michael Scanlan, T.O.R.
with James Manney

WHAT DOES
GOD
WANT?

A Practical Guide to Making Decisions

FRANCISCAN UNIVERSITY PRESS
Franciscan University of Steubenville
Steubenville, Ohio

Our Sunday Visitor Publishing Division
Our Sunday Visitor, Inc.
200 Noll Plaza
Huntington, Indiana 46750

ISBN: 0-87973-584-8
LCCCN: 95-71709

Cover design by: Peggy Leslie
PRINTED IN THE UNITED STATES OF AMERICA
584

Contents

Preface

"Will you give me your life?"

These words stopped me in my tracks one March morning in 1954 as I was returning home from Mass in Cambridge, Massachusetts. I stood paralyzed on the path I was taking across Henry Wadsworth Longfellow's estate. I knew God was speaking to me. I had never heard God speak to me that way before, but I knew it was Him.

I didn't answer immediately. I knew why. I was asking myself, "If I say 'Yes,' what will He do with my life?" I didn't want to answer this way because I did not want to refuse God or be ungrateful to Him. I also thought this a moment of grace; I didn't want to lose an opportunity that might pass and not return.

Finally, I struggled out a "Yes." But I cautiously added, "Can I wait to give you my life until I finish law school and pass the bar?" This seemed to be acceptable to God.

That short exchange changed my life. From then on I was committed to seeking God's will for my life. It was to be His life, not mine. Yet I had to make the decisions. From that day on, I began a struggle to order my life according to God's plan.

When I passed the bar, God let me know that he wanted me to be a priest. There followed eight difficult months of discerning where and when I should study for the priesthood. I knew the goal. But I had to decide how to get there.

Father Avery Dulles, S.J., my spiritual director through this time of struggle, gave me a principle that ultimately led to the peace and security of finding God's will for my life. He said the call was a restless spirit. When I found the place where the spirit could be poured out, leaving me at peace, I would have found the place where I should commit my life.

I found a place to pour out my restless spirit when I visited the Franciscan T.O.R. friars in Loretto, Pennsylvania. I entered that community in September, 1957. Now, nearly forty years later, I am still at peace, certain that I am living God's call for my life.

In those years, thousands of people — men and women, young and old, married, single, and religious — have asked me for guidance in making decisions. Some of the decisions are basic life vocations, such as my own call to the priesthood. Many more are decisions people make in the course of living out their vocation.

This book distills what I have learned in those years of making decisions and helping others make them. I hope it will help you find the true path of freedom and peace, which is to discern God's will — and to do it.

These are some scripture passages that have inspired me in making decisions in my life. I often return to them.

> Make known to me your ways, LORD;
> teach me your paths.
> Guide me in your truth and teach me,
> for you are God my savior.
> For you I wait all the long day.
>
> Ps 25:4-5

> Jesus said to them, "My food is to do the will of the one who sent me."
>
> Jn 4:34

No disciple is above his teacher....

Mt 10:24

Your will be done, on earth as in heaven.

Mt 6:10

I hope these passages guide you in your decisions. They guide the pages that follow, as I set out an approach to making decisions. Ultimately, a point comes when all those who persevere are able to let go of their lives and fall into God's will. I hope this book will help you reach that point in His grace.

Introduction

People who study such things say we make about a thousand choices a day. Perhaps two hundred of these are conscious decisions — or barely conscious. We make most of them without much thought, according to habit, expedience, or previous decisions. They are governed by the virtues of prudence and common sense.

Some of these decisions are more complex and require thought and prayer.

Perhaps your whole life is wrapped up in wrestling with one Big Decision — whether to marry the woman or man you've been dating, to leave the job you've been doing for fifteen years, to adopt a child, to fire someone who is working for you, to go to graduate school, to join a religious order.

Or you are struggling with smaller but still difficult choices — how to balance the family budget, whether to accept an invitation to serve on a committee at church, whether to ask that woman out a second (or third or fourth) time, how to balance work, family, and personal time.

Or an idea has come to you about making a change in your life. It may have come in prayer, through the suggestion of a friend, or perhaps it just popped into your mind one afternoon and won't go away. Is it from God? How do you know?

The idea may in fact be a deep yearning or desire that does not express itself in precise words. Frequently it will be persistent, almost imprisoning. You want to settle the matter by determining whether it is God's call.

"I have this desire to be a priest, but I am not that spiritual and I'm attracted to girls. And I always thought I would be an engineer."

"I want to be a physician. I'm doing well in my pre-med program. Now I have this desire to get married and I'm serious about this guy. I could put off the career thing until I see what happens with having children."

These are examples of deep desires. They are proper subjects for discernment even if the desire cannot be expressed clearly, indeed, even if your heart seems divided about the alternatives.

What does *God* want?

This book is designed to help you make that decision. It offers five tests to apply to a proposed course of action. They ask you to judge its *conformity* to God's revealed will, its contribution to the ongoing *conversion* of your heart, its *consistency* with the way God has led you in the past, how or whether it is *confirmed*, and the degree of *conviction* in your heart about the rightness of the decision.

I have formulated these tests through more than thirty years of experience of making my own decisions and helping others to make theirs. I have also drawn on the classic works about decision-making and discernment in the Catholic tradition. Despite all the assistance I have received from colleagues, friends, and the Catholic spiritual masters, the formulation of these tests is exclusively my responsibility.

I believe this book offers something that the many other Christian books on discernment and decision-making do not.

Catholic literature on discernment consists of two types. The first emphasizes the disciplines and habits of general growth in the spiritual life. The second type is aimed at spiritual directors. Both are useful. In fact, I have listed several good books from each category in the bibliography because many readers of this book may want to consult them. But this book, in contrast with most others, is as practical as my years of experience can make it. It is designed to help readers with decisions that are upon them *now*.

The Protestant evangelical literature on guidance tends to be practical but limited. It emphasizes scriptural norms and the importance of the spiritual anointing of the heart. It does not place decision-making in a context of Christian tradition and the authoritative teaching of the Church — essential elements for Catholics.

I believe this book will prove to be very helpful to many readers, but I also know it is limited. I am not wise enough, nor spiritually mature enough, to write something that will be completely adequate for everyone. Circumstances are different for each individual. Therefore, I strongly urge the counsel of a spiritual director for those Big Decisions which involve life commitments or which would have serious negative consequences if made poorly.

I have tried to make this book as usable as possible. This is the way I approach decisions. This is the way I counsel others to approach theirs. If you apply these five tests prayerfully, in a spirit of submission to the Lord and openness to the Holy Spirit, you are likely to come to know the answer to the question: *What does **God** want?*

The tests do not have to be followed in a precise order. The order given here is the one that I believe has been most efficient in my experience — that is, as the way that leads to a decision in the shortest time and with the greatest clarity.

The tests are:

Conformity - to God's revealed will.

Conversion

Consistency

Confirmation

Conviction

Chapter 1
Does It Conform to God's Will?

Sandra and Peter knew each other slightly from activities at St. Thomas More parish, but they became fast friends when they were both cast for parts in a musical at their local civic theater. They spent rehearsal breaks together. Often the breaks were very long. They began to car pool. They shared deeply about their pasts, their vision for their lives, their hopes. They shared their disappointments. Sandra was divorced; Peter was married to a woman who was addicted to prescription drugs. Sandra and Peter were especially interested in spiritual matters. The friendship was important for both of them. They came to rely on each other for personal support. They also shared a strong Catholic faith.

One night after a very long rehearsal, Peter gave Sandra a ride home. They each sensed something electric in the air. By the time they arrived at Sandra's apartment, they knew it was a feeling of powerful mutual sexual attraction. Sandra asked Peter if he wanted to come in for a drink. He put his arm around her. Then they pulled back. "Is this right?" they both said at the same time. They looked at each other with desire. They were both thinking, "This is so good. How can it be wrong?"

The first test for Catholic discernment is the test of conformity. This doesn't mean conformity to your passions or conformity to peer group pressures. It is difficult to "conform" one-self to these things because passions and pressures come and go. By definition, they are changeable. Rather, I mean conformity to God's revealed will. He has already spoken about many of the choices and dilemmas that human beings face. In other places His revealed will does not address our problems directly, but His teaching presents a clear path for us that makes the task of discernment and decision-making easier. The main sources for this teaching are scripture, tradition, and the teaching of the Church.

Peter and Sandra are at the point of deciding whether they should have a sexual relationship. The answer is not difficult. Adultery and fornication break God's law. Few teachings in scripture and the moral teaching of the Church are clearer and more consistent. You and I, examining their situation with detachment, can see this. Peter and Sandra probably know this too.

But it's quite possible that Peter and Sandra see their situation as a knotty conflict of goods rather than as temptation to be avoided. It is their pleasure and communication versus Catholic teaching on the proper place of sex. Making love "wouldn't hurt anybody." This is the attitude they encounter every day at work — and in the civic theater group.

Being faithful to God's will for them is going to be very difficult even though they probably know what it is. They are in the throes of sexual desire, at a time and place where temptation is at its most powerful. Nothing is stopping them from going to bed together; much is telling them to go ahead.

There's a saying in politics: Timing is everything. That's not completely true in the moral life, but timing does count for a lot. On one level, Peter and Sandra's discernment question is a no-brainer. They should go home — separately. But their timing is very poor. The best time to apply the conformity test was weeks earlier, when they sensed a mutual attraction and found themselves becoming emotionally involved.

Our little vignette raises another pitfall in discernment. We leave Peter and Sandra wondering how something so good can be so wrong. We are often tempted to justify or rationalize sin. We can tell ourselves that the morally right course is ambiguous even when it's not, that we're merely choosing between two good alternatives. Christian discernment can become difficult and uncertain when it shouldn't be.

To speak of "conformity to God's law" has an unpleasant ring to many modern ears: a matter of grimly obeying rules and regulations from moral theology texts and Vatican documents. Conformity does involve obedience — sometimes obedience for its own sake. Often we conform ourselves reluctantly, with a measure of struggle, and with wishes that it could be different. But the point of scripture and the teaching of the Church is to make us free. The laws we conform to are rooted in an understanding of how human beings are put together, how human society works, how we are to live so we fulfill our obligations to others and to God. Transgressing these principles imprisons us. It limits our choices; it stunts our growth. Living in faithfulness to them brings us peace and joy.

Peter and Sandra's situation illustrates this aspect of conformity to God's will. It doesn't take a rocket scientist to see how a passionate extra-marital affair could bring misery to Peter and Sandra and to many other people besides. They should go to their own homes, not just out of obedience to a law, but for the sake of their own integrity and freedom.

The conformity test asks us to compare our proposed decision, commitment, journey, or action to the will of God for His people as revealed in scripture, tradition, and the authoritative teaching of the Catholic Church. Often this will be relatively simple. It may require some reading — the *Catechism of the Catholic Church*, perhaps, or a good commentary on scripture. Sometimes the conformity test requires a discussion with a knowledgeable spiritual director or other pastor.

The test will yield one of three conclusions:
- The decision, or commitment, or action is in conformity with God's law and the teaching of the Church. It should be further examined with the other tests.
- The proposed action is not in conformity with God's law and the teaching of the Church. It should be rejected as something not of God.
- The proposed action is in part compatible and in part not compatible. Further examination is needed.

Barbara was a twenty-eight-year-old widow with two young children. She was falling in love with Chris, a young man who had been divorced. Chris and Barbara had a deep spiritual life together — deeper than either had had with their previous partners. Both were active participants in a charismatic prayer group. Chris was a powerful youth leader. He often received prophetic words and led others by the sheer power of his charismatic personality. Chris was urging marriage. He was sure the Lord wanted him and Barbara to be married. He could support Barbara and her children in comfort. She could stay at home with the children instead of working full-time. The problem was Chris's former marriage. He had been civilly divorced; an annulment was pending.

Barbara thought this was a conflict of goods. It would be good for her to have a Christian husband, good for her children to have a father, good for her to stay at home instead of working. Chris's inspiration both excited her and disturbed her. Was he right? Did the Lord want them to be married? What about his previous marriage? In some confusion, she went to see her pastor.

I told Barbara that she should not consider marrying Chris until the annulment was granted, *if* it was granted. This was the application of the conformity test. Once the marriage was possible in the eyes of the Church, then she could proceed to weigh the other factors that enter into a decision as serious as marriage. Until then, I said, put the relationship on hold. I actually went further. I advised her to stop discussing marriage with Chris and to cool off the relationship until the Church decided the annulment.

Barbara was afraid the annulment wouldn't come. I urged her to see that possibility as a revelation of God's will for her if it happened. Her family's welfare was important, but her obedience to God, her surrender to His will, was more important. And she would not be abandoned by God and her friends if she didn't marry Chris. Love of God and Church goes before love of self and one's plans.

I told Barbara that deeper trust in God's providence follows submission and obedience. I advised her to intensify her prayer for God's provision for her family, and trust Him more fully than ever before.

I suggested to Barbara that she ignore Chris's conviction that the Lord wanted him and Barbara to be married. The conformity test is a good way to identify false prophecies and false inspirations, which often happens among lay leaders in the Church who have built strong ministries. They are accustomed to seeking and following inspirations of the Holy Spirit. They are praised for their accomplishments in building a ministry. They grow very confident in their ability to lead others and discern what the Lord wants. Without accountability and a healthy prayer life, such leaders can succumb to the temptation to disguise their own desires in religious language.

I might add that charismatic leaders are not the only ones who are subject to dubious interior senses of what the Lord wants them to do. Many people are, including those who take their relationship with the Lord very seriously.

Barbara's unfinished story shows us how the conformity test can help simplify the process of decision-making. For now, decisions about Chris's convictions, the couple's compatibility, the romantic element, financial security, and common vision for marriage can all be deferred.

Sometimes divine "leadings" seem to be confirmed by signs. The conformity test is valuable here too.

Ted, a man with a wife and five school-age children, told me that he had a persistent, strong call to enter the Franciscan religious life. He thought this call had been confirmed by "signs." He had prayed for a Bible passage and received the story of Jesus telling the rich young man to sell all he had and follow him. A childhood friend, a Capuchin Franciscan whom he had not seen for years, suddenly began a correspondence with him. He turned on the TV on a whim one night and the movie "Francis of Assisi" popped up on the screen. He was confused. His wife was nearly distraught.

The conformity test helped us rule out religious life. Religious life is a good thing, but it wasn't an option for him. His first responsibility before God was for his wife and family. But the conformity test also helped identify what God really wanted Ted to do. I thought Ted had a valid call; it was just misdirected to the religious life. The Lord was calling him to a greater sacrificial service — but to his family and community. Ted came to see that the Franciscan "signs" he received were calls to assume the energy and selflessness of St. Francis as he served his wife and children.

St. Francis of Assisi is a great model of a man who sought above all to conform himself to God's will. As a young man he was a soldier who quested after military glory. He heard the Lord in a dream ask him, "Is it better to serve the servant or the master?" "The master," he replied. The Lord asked, "Then why do you follow the servant?" Francis withdrew from the military life and became a penitent.

Later he heard the Lord from the cross in the San Damiano Church say to him, "Rebuild my church which as you see around you is falling down." Francis took this command literally and spent time repairing the walls of churches. When men came to him and asked to join as disciples, Francis then understood that he was to rebuild with living stones — human beings.

At Mass one day Francis heard the priest proclaim the gospel, "Go, sell what you have and give it to the poor and come follow me." Francis understood this as God's direction to him. He embraced poverty as the distinctive mark of his life and the Franciscan order — so much so that he and the first friars spoke of "Lady Poverty" as a noble lady to be embraced and wed. This developed into a rule of life for the friars.

Each call built on an earlier one. Francis responded to each call with a spirit of submitting to God, conforming to His will, obeying His law, following His Gospel. Francis so truly conformed that he has been proclaimed through the ages as the most Christ-like of men.

Carolyn, a lawyer three months out of law school, received a letter inviting her to interview for what looked like the perfect job. It was a large firm in Washington, D.C., the city she wanted to live in. They had reviewed her work. They had checked references. She looked like someone they wanted, the partner in charge of recruitment wrote.

The interview with the partner went very well. At the end, Carolyn asked about the firm's clients. The partner handed her a list. About five names from the top was the name Planned Parenthood of America. "Planned Parenthood does a lot of abortions, doesn't it?" Carolyn asked. "You bet. And they get sued and they sue back," said the partner. "A lot of legal work. They're one of our biggest cli-

ents." Then he narrowed his eyes and looked at Carolyn carefully. "You don't have a problem with that, do you?"

Carolyn did have a problem. But what kind of problem? Applying the conformity test in Carolyn's case required some interpretation. No combination of scripture passages, encyclicals, and moral teaching says directly that a Catholic shouldn't work for a law firm that counts Planned Parenthood as one of its most valued clients. In fact, the moral teaching of the Church contains relatively few specific prohibitions. We are to form our conscience according to the teaching of the Church and then act in accordance with this conscience.

The Church has spoken very clearly and consistently about abortion. The direct killing of innocent life is always a grave wrong. Catholics are prohibited from having abortions, performing abortions, working where abortions are performed, and promoting abortions.

But did it follow that Carolyn should turn down the job? She didn't want to cooperate with evil, but was this really cooperation? What if she could be insulated from Planned Parenthood and do other work for the firm? She asked the partner for time to think; she turned these questions over in her mind as she returned home after the interview. At times she wished the Church had made her decision for her by issuing a rule for people in situations like hers.

In the end, Carolyn said no. She thought she *could* pursue the matter further and see if it were possible to work out an acceptable arrangement. But she thought there was a real danger in getting entangled in evil. For her, the job didn't pass the conformity test.

Carolyn acted in a spirit of obedience to the spirit of Catholic teaching. Her story underscores an important aspect of Church teaching: We are not stifling our "true" selves when we act in a spirit of submission and obedience. Rather, we become freer and more fully who we are: sons and daughters of God, members of his family. And obeying merely the letter of the law is not enough. The *spirit* of obedience and submission is crucial. Carolyn is free of dubious compromise and implication in evil. Even more, she is a free woman who has freely chosen to follow the Lord.

When making decisions, ask yourself this question: Am I truly seeking to be under God's authority and serve Him and His Church? If so, vow not to evade the letter or the spirit of the law. Stand under the law and the Lawgiver, striving to be neither excessively strict nor excessively loose in interpretation, conforming in every way to the mind of the Lord and the Church.

The freedom of living in conformity is immense. This is what we were created for, and, as Pope John Paul II teaches powerfully in *Veritatis Splendor*, our very being finds freedom in becoming who we are when we obey God's law. We join the prophets of old who said, "Here I am, Lord, I have come to do your will." We join our mother Mary, as she says, "Behold the handmaid of the Lord. Fiat! Magnificat!" In the oft-repeated saying of Mother Teresa, "The gospel says nothing about success, only faithfulness." True success comes through faithfulness.

This is the encouragement we can all have as we struggle to be honest in business when those around us are cheating, to be pure when our friends are involved in immoral relationships, to be truthful on tax returns when accountants are encouraging false reports, to forgo revenge when someone has badly wronged us, to be faithful in the many commitments we've made when pressures mount to get out of them. Faithfulness is a way of life.

The religious life is a special kind of commitment and it requires special efforts to be faithful to it. Discernment within religious life can present unusual complexities; more people can be involved in a decision than with lay people, and procedures can be lengthy. But many in the religious life have a great advantage — the vow of obedience.

When I was in the seminary, I was convinced I was called to the foreign missions. I had a great interest in missions and a heart for the work. I was president of the mission club in seminary. I regularly told my superiors that I was applying for missions in Brazil.

At ordination time, I came to my minister provincial for assignment. He said he had a better use for me — in college administration. I was shocked. I thought I had been following God's call in pursuing missions and now the man with authority over me was directing me down a completely different path.

My vow of obedience settled the matter at the time. I went into college administration. I was permitted to make an annual petition for the missions. I did this for ten consecutive years; each year it was rejected. Finally, when I was president of the College of Steubenville, I was asked to withdraw my name from any further consideration. I did.

At this moment, it was clear to me that God had never called me to the missions. College administration was where God wanted me to be. I would not have been as fruitful or as happy as a missionary. I had wanted a more heroic life, and my desire had settled on the missions. In reality, I could live a life of great heroism and virtue right where I was — in Steubenville, Ohio.

My vow of obedience helped me then. But the principle applies to every Christian: The spirit of obedience is a crucial part of our efforts to hear the Lord and follow His will. It's not enough to conform merely to the letter of the law. What's required of us is an eagerness to be under God's authority and to serve Him and His Church.

We have seen how the conformity test can rule out some courses of action and ratify others. Sometimes, however, the test doesn't give a clear answer, even when we have to make very important decisions.

When his company gave him a laptop computer he could take home, Paul gladly automated the family finances after years of paper figuring. But technology didn't change the facts. It only displayed them more vividly in full color: The Borczaks were gradually going broke. Paul's salary did not cover the very tight monthly budget. Each month they dipped into savings to buy some necessities. The budget did not contain money for the car they badly needed, or for school tuition next fall, or for a new roof, furnace replacement, gifts, vacation, and other "extras."

Paul and Connie agreed that they had to do something. Could Paul get a second job? That would be hard for a man who worked long hours in the construction business. A new job? Maybe eventually, but the industry was anticipating recession and companies weren't hiring. "Should I work?" Connie asked. She was a social worker. Connie stayed home with their three children, aged seven, five, and three. Paul and Connie were very reluctant to use day care. When they were married, they agreed that Connie would not work outside the house while the children were young.

They talked far into the night. Connie knew of several full-time social work jobs. Part-time jobs for social workers were much scarcer. Would an hourly part-time job be worth it? What would this do to their marriage? What would it do to the children? Would the additional income outweigh the harm to the children without their mother around? "I wish I knew what the Lord wanted," Paul said. As she fell asleep, Connie said she thought so too.

What Does *God* Want?

If anything, scripture and Church teaching make the Borczaks' dilemma more acute. They tell us that parents have a responsibility to make adequate material provision for their children. They also tell us we must provide love and care and responsible training for them. Here these responsibilities are in apparent conflict. They often are. We aren't the first generation in history to be burdened by conflicts between providing materially for a family and providing adequate nurturing. In fact, this dilemma was worse for most people in the past, when people worked harder for less.

Many of our most difficult decisions resemble Paul and Connie's. We are faced with choices to pursue one good at the expense of another and to settle for something less than the ideal. Where should I spend my volunteer time? How much volunteer work is "enough"? Should I take three difficult courses in a semester or fewer so I can get higher grades? Is it better to leave my current job because the atmosphere in the office is so terrible or should I work to change the atmosphere?

Paul and Connie have not decided on a proposed course of action, so they cannot as yet "test" it. It's clear, however, that the conformity test is likely to be inconclusive. Both the couple's goals — financial solvency and a strong family life — are admirable, fortified by a strong desire to be Catholic parents of a Catholic family. Both are approaching the problem in a spirit of sacrifice and obedience. It's likely that whatever they decide will involve a compromise; they will have to settle for some resolution of the problem that will be less than ideal.

They will have to turn to the other tests of discernment.

Summary

Does It Conform to God's Will?

1. Relevant commandments of God

2. Relevant teachings of the Church

3. Existing commitments that bear on the decision (work, family, etc.)

4. Existing "calls" from God that might contradict the current proposal

5. Might the current proposal hinder a spirit of submission and obedience to God and His Church?

Conclusions about conformity

Chapter 2
Does It Encourage Conversion?

Evelyn and Gina had taken different paths after leaving college, where they had been roommates. Evelyn was raising a family in Florida; Gina was living the high life in Manhattan. She had succeeded spectacularly as a marketing executive, earning a six-figure salary before she was thirty. She lived in a condo on the East Side and had bought a summer place on Long Island Sound. She vacationed in the Caribbean and Vail, and traveled to Europe and Mexico. She dressed expensively and drove a nifty white Mercedes sports car when out of the city. When they got together for their yearly meeting, Gina showed off her latest possessions, but she also complained about how deeply in debt she was. In fact, she talked mainly about money — and about cheap, greedy men.

At their latest get-together, Gina told Evelyn that she had had several serious bouts of depression. She talked about a job dilemma. She was being wooed by an ad agency in Hong Kong. More money. Exotic surroundings. But she really didn't want to leave New York.

"What would you do, Ev?" she asked.

Every decision we make, all the work we do, every relationship we enter into, should draw us closer to the Lord. "Conversion" is one word we use to describe this process. Another is "holiness." The first test of decision-making involved the rightness and wrongness of an action: Is the proposed decision in conformity to God's will as already revealed? The second test looks at the heart. Will the proposed action draw us closer to God or lead us away from Him?

In one sense, the test of conversion is the only one that matters. The whole point of the Christian life is to love God and to prepare ourselves to be with Him for eternity. In Luke's Gospel we read about the lawyer who rose to pose a question: What must I do to inherit everlasting life? Jesus asked him to repeat what was written in the law: "…You shall love the Lord, your God, with all your heart, with all your being, with all your strength, and with all your mind, and your neighbor as yourself" (Lk 10:27).

In his letter to Titus, Paul describes what a holy life should look like. "For the grace of God has appeared, saving all and training us to reject godless ways and worldly desires and to live temperately, justly, and devoutly in this age, as we await the blessed hope, the appearance of the glory of the great God and our savior Jesus Christ" (Ti 2:11-12).

One other gospel passage is directly relevant to Christian decision-making. It is from Jesus' prayer in Chapter 12 of John: "Whoever loves his life loses it, and whoever hates his life in this world will preserve it for eternal life. Whoever serves me must follow me, and where I am, there also will my servant be" (Jn 12:25-26).

Scripture teaches that holiness is not something abstract or theoretical. It involves our daily lives (living "temperately, justly, and devoutly in this age"). It can also be difficult; we emulate Jesus, the seed that dies and produces much fruit. Holiness doesn't descend on us, like a cloud of glory from heaven. We grow in it, through trouble and challenge, over obstacles and opposition — by God's grace.

Conversion is a process of becoming a certain kind of person through the decisions, commitments, and achievements of one's life. The word "conversion" suggests a turning to God and away from the darkness of sin. But conversion can actually apply to any disposition of the heart. We can be converted to evil as well as to good. I've known good Christians who have become converted to New Age paganism. I've watched student radicals become crooked businessmen. I've seen women consumed by the ideology of radical feminism and men seduced by the darkness of the homosexual subculture.

The world is full of ideas and pleasures and values that tug at our hearts. We are always being converted from something old to something new. We must make sure that our decisions — large and small — direct our hearts along the path to God.

This path can be hard to find on occasion. Our resolve to walk it can waver. All of us will make mistakes. Nevertheless, Gina doesn't appear to be on the path to God at all. At best, it is a long-neglected ideal that has little practical reality in her life. The emptiness of her way of life — its show, its glamor, its grounding in acquisitive materialism — is already having a destructive effect on this young woman. If Evelyn is close enough to her, and if Gina is receptive, Evelyn may be able to raise some of these deeper spiritual questions. But one thing's for sure: A move to a better job in Hong Kong won't help Gina very much. Unless she reexamines the direction of her life, a decision to stay in New York won't help either.

The conversion test is especially important when we are presented with choices involving more money, more power, more public attention, more fame. Will this choice turn my heart to God? Does it present any special dangers to me? What are my motives for pursuing it? Will the risks overwhelm the benefits?

I have faced my share of decisions of this kind. I have often found it difficult to determine why I am interested in a role of greater influence and visibility. This has usually been a harder test to apply than the conformity test. Let us look at some of the criteria that can help us grow closer to the Lord in the decisions we make.

Two years earlier Elliott and Mary Ann had asked their oldest son, Neil, to leave home. It was a "tough love" situation, and they ached with grief and regret. Neil used drugs heavily and dropped out of high school. He had wrecked two cars. Twice the police had picked him up wandering around town in a stupor. The police suspected him of dealing drugs as well as using them. Life at home with Neil was intolerable. He alternately fought with his younger brothers and introduced them to his friends. So, in tears and sorrow, after an agonizing inner debate, Elliott and Mary Ann showed him the door.

Neil surprised everyone by getting and keeping two hourly, low-wage jobs. Then he got his high school equivalency diploma. He came to the house for pleasant visits. He said he was off drugs and wanted to make something of himself. Neil still looked unkempt — "like a guitarist in a grunge band," Elliott growled — but he had definitely changed for the better. Now Neil wanted to move back home so he could cut down on expenses and attend the local community college.

The request caught his parents by surprise. Mary Ann was inclined to say no. Elliott wanted to say yes. It was a terrible risk, she said. We might be able to help him, he replied. Only Neil can help Neil, Mary Ann said. Besides, think of the other boys. They talked for a long time. At one point, Mary Ann and Elliott switched positions, she favoring the move, he growing skeptical about it. They had rarely been so perplexed about any decision in their entire marriage.

One of the first standards for determining the rightness of a course of action is to look at the probable results and, if possible, the results of similar decisions in the past. Has the decision led to more productive and satisfying work, happier and more secure family members and associates, a richer prayer life, growth in virtue? When considering several courses of action, does one seem to point to these qualities more directly than the others? We Americans are known for our pragmatism. We shouldn't have trouble looking at the results.

The biblical word for results is "fruit." Jesus' own saying— "by their fruit you shall know them" — is one of the world's best-known aphorisms. For good reason. When inspecting a tree, you judge its fruit. When considering a man — a potential spouse, a possible new boss, a presidential candidate — you look at the fruit. Are his actions consistent with his values? Does he do good? Does he do what he says he will do? The tree might be gnarled and misshapen. The man might not be terribly handsome. But if they bear good fruit, it's likely they are good too. As Duke Ellington once said about music, "If it sounds good, it *is* good."

Judging the fruit of decisions usually involves assessing someone's action. Talk is important, but talk is also cheap (to quote an aphorism *not* coined by Jesus). Elliott and Mary Ann are considering taking their son back home only because Neil has shown by his actions that something fundamental may have changed for him. Holding two jobs and finishing high school on his own are indisputably good things. Many things could still go wrong for him, but his parents are primarily looking at what he has *done* rather than what he has *said*.

A man once came to me to tell me about his conviction that the Lord wanted him to do public battle with a small lay ministry that he thought was doing terrible damage to the Church. He wanted to attack the leaders in print, denounce them to the bishop, and make secret contact with ministry workers and urge them to quit. This man was a former and thoroughly disaffected staff member of this ministry.

He had a dozen reasons why the program was a menace and he explained them eloquently. He spoke passionately about protecting the Church. I listened, then offered some suggestions for other ways to approach the problem. He resisted them. I realized that he was bent on revenge. His proposed course of action was meant to harm individuals and ruin their reputations. He said that might be a by-product of righting wrongs. I saw that, for this man, doing damage was the main goal.

When making decisions, we can also look at the fruit of past decisions. I know a middle-aged woman on the West Coast who recently went to some expense and considerable trouble to take an adult education course in marketing at a local college. When I asked her why (she doesn't hold a job that requires marketing knowledge), she said that she had taken many evening courses over the years and that they had always stimulated her mind. "They've been good for me," she said.

As they discuss their tough decision about Neil, Elliott and Mary Ann not only look ahead at the probable fruit of saying yes or no about his request to come home. They can also look at the fruit of their earlier decision to ask him to leave. It seems to have borne good fruit — a more peaceful home and positive changes in Neil. They still have many factors to weigh, but they can have confidence in their ability to discern what is best for their family.

Talk is cheap and actions speak louder than words. Actions are rooted in the dispositions of our hearts. This is the real fruit. Paul describes the fruit of the Spirit as "love, joy, peace, patience, kindness, generosity, faithfulness, gentleness, self-control" (Gal 5:22). All of these are virtues that grow in relationships. So are the works of the flesh, some of which Paul also names: "Let us not become conceited, provoking one another, envious of one another" (Gal 5:26). Pride, aggression, and envy are lined up against love, joy, and peace.

Henry had been hired to support the company's
complex computer system. Stan, his boss, had to

admit that Henry was technically brilliant. He worked methodically and patiently to fix system glitches and to install new software. He frequently hit on innovative solutions to problems that had eluded others. But Henry had no patience with people. He hung up the phone on his "clients," argued with his colleagues, and neglected administrative chores. But he always came to work and he worked very hard.

Henry's three-month new employee probation had a month to go. He had a few supporters among those who had benefitted from his technical genius. But most people in the office disliked him. Some insisted that Stan get rid of him. Stan was inclined to let Henry go. "I might not be able to replace him with someone as bright," he reasoned, "but life will sure be a lot easier around here."

When applying the conversion test, it is not always easy to discern what fruits are likely to grow from a particular course of action. A bad tree can give off what appears to be good fruit. Some people work hard to disguise their true motives. Most dangerously, we hide our real intentions even from ourselves. We can deceive ourselves into thinking that a decision is correct because "everything seems to line up," when in reality the person is simply being carried along by events. Even worse, we can rationalize something that serves our own interests by deciding that it is the Lord's will.

Stan is faced with a decision that presents these dangers. The facts are subject to varying interpretations. Stan's responsibilities seem to conflict. He has to get his department's work done, keep peace among the staff, and be fair to Henry. And, of course, he wants his own life to be as pleasant and trouble-free as possible. It is, in short, a situation in which Stan can find reasons to do whatever he wants to do.

We've been in his shoes. Should I put more into this job or take it easy? Should I keep up a relationship with an old but difficult friend? Isn't it time to be a little extravagant and buy that sports car I've always wanted? Should I fire that troublesome employee and have things go a little easier for me for a change? These choices are not necessarily bad fruit. But they are not necessarily the fruit the Lord wants to grow from our decisions.

Christians often approach decisions with what looks like a carefree attitude, saying something like, "If the Lord wants to stop me, He has plenty of chances to do it." Should I buy this big new house in a fine neighborhood? Well, look how many ways the Lord can stop me: the owners can refuse my offer; they can refuse my counteroffer; financing can fall through; the inspector can find termites; the survey can turn up a problem; we can fail to reach a final agreement on the cost of repairs; I might not get the raise I was counting on to handle the larger mortgage payments.

Job change? Negotiations can break down and all kinds of other obstacles are possible. The Lord can use any of them. Going back to school? I might do poorly on the Graduate Record tests. The school might not admit me. I might not find the money.

The Lord can and does stop us by closing doors. But the "Lord-can-stop-me" approach can disguise a wilfulness on our part to do something that we are determined to do at most any cost. It can also disguise failure to truly examine the alternatives.

It's important to make a *decision*. Sometimes the right decision means breaking with the flow of events, making people uncomfortable, causing upset. Paul, for example, wrote some of his epistles primarily to correct serious problems in the early church communities. It's probable that his letters *increased* tensions in these churches. In the long run, they promoted peace and good fellowship, but in the shorter term the fruit might have been fiercer controversy, sharper division, and a harvest of hurt feelings.

What Does *God* Want?

It may be right for Stan to let Henry go. But he should make a *decision* to do so in light of all the considerations in force — not simply to drift in that direction because it "seems right," a direction that incidently seems best for Stan.

It may also be right for Stan to keep Henry, to work with him to change his behavior and take flack from people who are offended by him. This may be fairer to Henry and best for Stan's department in the long run. But this is a tougher course. If Stan goes this way — against the flow — he needs to make a decision to do that too.

Immaculate Conception was an old parish in a decaying urban neighborhood. Membership had dropped by fifty percent in three years. Staff had been laid off. The diocese had to subsidize the budget. The future looked grim, but the parish was beloved by many in the neighborhood and it ran many programs that served the community.

It still came as a shock to the pastor, Father George, when the bishop summoned him to his office, put a hand on his shoulder, and told him that Immaculate Conception was going to be closed. The curtain was to go down in three months. It was the worst three months of Father George's life. At the end he realized that closing Immaculate Conception had taken a severe personal toll. So he took a couple of months off.

Father George had always had a fruitful prayer life, not without periods of dryness, but consistent and satisfying. Now, however, it seemed to Father George as if God had suddenly abandoned him. This was different from any problem in prayer he had had before — as if God had pushed him off a cliff into a terrifying abyss and was watching him fall.

He felt an overpowering sense of betrayal. And a crushing loneliness. He felt that God had left him alone. That was the hardest thing for Father George to take.

He sought out his spiritual director, the prior of a community of Benedictines. He described his situation and asked, "What's happening to me?"

The priest's spiritual director must consider several possibilities for the source of Father George's distress. He has suffered a great loss in the closing of his beloved parish. This deep emotional blow might go a long way toward explaining his desolation. He might even benefit from some professional counseling that would help him understand how to express grief.

But these trials might also be a normal — and important — step in spiritual growth. Those who desire "to put on Christ Jesus" are promised pruning and purification. St. Teresa of Avila, St. John of the Cross, and many other great spiritual writers guarantee dryness and desolation on the way to holiness and union with God. If an experience of distress, abandonment, desolation, or persecution occurs at a time when a major change is taking place, careful discernment is needed. Perhaps the person should pull back from the new direction. But then again this might be a time of purification that calls for steadfastness.

Prayer is the gateway to conversion. It is through prayer that we receive that inner revelation of where we stand before God and what He is calling us to be. Prayer is how He is calling us to be holy.

In my life and in the lives of many whom I have directed, scripture has been particularly important to applying the conversion test. Reading and praying through Holy Scripture gives us God's perspective. We can find disciples of the Lord in the Old and New Testament that we can identify with. The Holy Spirit lives in scripture. That is why we say scripture is *in-*

spired. As we read scripture, desiring to learn from it, the Holy Spirit becomes active in our lives.

It is often helpful to write down insights and words that we experience while reading scripture. As we review and reflect on these words, we will gradually form a clearer picture of the way God is calling us to holiness. Each time we pray over a passage, we open to the possibility of God revealing deeper meaning in it for our lives.

One passage in my notebook that I often return to when praying for a deeper conversion is from a letter written by St. Ignatius of Antioch to Christians in Rome while he was preparing for his martyrdom. Ignatius did not want his fellow Christians to interfere with the glory the Lord had in store for him:

> I am writing to all the churches to let it be known that I will gladly die for God if only you do not stand in my way. I plead with you: show me no untimely kindness. Let me be food for the wild beasts, for they are my way to God. I am God's wheat and shall be ground by their teeth so that I may become Christ's pure bread. Pray to Christ for me that the animals will be the means of making me a sacrificial victim for God.

Summary

Does It Encourage Conversion?

1. Will the proposed direction lead to a closer union with God?

2. Will the proposed direction lead to a more faithful discharge of my primary responsibilities?

3. Does the proposal involve an unnecessary occasion of sin?

Conclusions about conversion

Chapter 3
Is It Consistent?

*Fernando came to see his spiritual director with
a plan that looked radical, even shocking. He wanted
to give away most of his assets to the Church. He
wanted to start an endowment for the Catholic school
system in the city where he lived, support some evan-
gelization work, provide for missionaries, and start
a Catholic-evangelical institute in a Catholic university. Fernando had the assets to do all this. After
fleeing Castro's Cuba in the early '60s, he had made
a fortune as a developer of shopping centers in
Florida and elsewhere in the South.*

*Fernando wasn't completely sure that this was
the right decision. He was afraid that his friends
would think he was crazy. His family wasn't entirely
with him either. His wife and three daughters were
well provided for, but they didn't share Fernando's
passion for Catholic projects. Still, they recognized
that he could do what he wanted with his money.
Was he being impulsive, extravagant, ruled by emotions? Giving his money away seemed like such an
extraordinary thing to do.*

*As they talked and prayed, Fernando and his
spiritual director saw that this step wasn't extraordinary in the context of Fernando's life. In the crucial moments of his life, he had felt called by God to
act boldly without knowing how his actions would
turn out. He felt a call to make a dangerous escape
from Cuba. He felt called to get married even though
he was virtually penniless. He followed the same type
of call as he entered a risky business and made many*

*bold decisions over the years as the business grew.
He had contributed generously to the Church for
many years. His habit had been to carefully assess
the Church projects he was interested in and then
turn over his money with no strings attached.*

*Fernando said, "My heart is pierced every time
I hear the story of the rich young man. Jesus says,
'Sell all that you have and give to the poor and come
follow me.' That's what I want to do."*

God is consistent. When He communicates with us, He usually does so in a familiar way, a way we will recognize. Sometimes we worry that we are going to miss His message. Decision-making, we sometimes think, is like being a batter up at the plate facing a crafty pitcher who is a master at keeping batters guessing. You don't know what to expect — fast ball, curve, slider, change-up; inside, outside, high, or low. God is more like the manager. He has a system of signs to communicate with His players on the field during a game. The players know what the signs mean — or they are supposed to. If they get confused, the Manager has other ways to make His wishes known.

God speaks to us consistently, but that doesn't mean that He always does the same things. He is leading Fernando to do something new, something that many outsiders are likely to perceive as outlandish. But He has dealt with Fernando in similar ways many times in the past. Fernando is accustomed to taking bold steps and supporting Catholic ministries. This new plan — striking as it is — is consistent with his past life. It would be unusual if the Lord directed Fernando to buy a baseball team or invest his wealth in safe Treasury bills. *That* would be a tricky slow curve to a batter waiting for a fast ball.

In the previous two chapters, we looked at the role of conformity and conversion in our decision-making. Our decisions need to conform to God's revealed will. They need to bring us and others toward conversion, toward greater love of God and surrender of our hearts. A third test is that of consistency. Does the option we are considering seem to fit the kind of person we are? Is it consistent with the way God has worked with us in the past? Has the Lord ever spoken to us this way before?

God's guidance is an essentially conservative process. His dealings with us are usually consistent with the way He has dealt with us in the past. His grace operates in concrete circumstances rather than in abstract conjectures. He speaks in a way we are accustomed to hear. And we will often find Him following a plan that unfolds over a period of years in which many decisions lead directly from those that precede them. In fact, the current possibility under consideration may be part of the unfolding of a larger plan that the Lord has previously set in motion and which you have already determined is His will. If so, your decision-making may be very simple. All you need do is determine whether the current direction is part of a larger plan.

A very important aspect of the consistency test is to examine the way you hear the Lord speaking to you. Is the current prompting coming in a way that you recognize from the past? You may be considering something brand new, as Fernando is doing. Or you may be taking the next step on a familiar path. In any case, the Lord is likely to lead you in a way that you can have confidence in because He has spoken to you that way before.

At least six times in my life, a loud knock on my door has awakened me from a deep sleep. I got up, opened the door, and found no one there. I went back to sleep only to be awakened by a loud knock again a short time later. The first three times this happened I went to sleep again, only to be awakened by the knock a third time.

Each time, however, I eventually got on my knees and said, "Speak, Lord, your servant is listening." I then experienced an inner sense or inner voice telling me something I needed to change in my life or something new I needed to do. I was able to see this as a probable word from the Lord for me, because the knock on the door in the middle of the night eventually became a pattern of His communication with me. It's not by any means the ordinary way He speaks to me about my life and work; it happens rarely. But when it happens I recognize it.

When I was younger, I often felt a strong sensory tumult when the Lord was about to communicate something important to me. I would get excited. I "knew" the Holy Spirit was surging about, stirring my heart, preparing me to receive something from God. My senses would seem sharper, my consciousness heightened. Christians sometimes call this experience an "anointing." Like the anointing that accompanied the making of a medieval knight, the anointing I felt as a young man signified God's special intervention in my life.

This happens less frequently now. More often I experience the Lord dealing with me through invitations, gently offered. I first experienced a divine invitation when I was in my first year of law school at Harvard. One chilly morning in Lent, as I was coming back home from Mass, I was suddenly stopped in my tracks as I crossed a park. Then the Lord spoke to me; I heard words within me saying, "Will you give me your whole life?" I was calm, not disturbed. I knew at the time that the question was from the Lord and I have never doubted it since. That moment was a turning point for me. Other invitations followed — to become a priest, a Franciscan, a university president, and other important changes. This is how I experience calls to make a major departure from what I am currently doing — invitations, not anointings, but clearly from God because I recognize that mode of communication.

Many people I counsel have heard the Lord in certain specific ways. A woman I know hears Him in the quiet moments after communion. He speaks words of guidance infrequently, but when He does, that is usually the time when He does it.

A man I have known for years almost always hears the Lord in a powerful fashion on his annual retreat — and rarely at other times. Others hear the Lord's guidance through the counsel of their spiritual directors or confessors. Some people "hear" the Lord; they will receive a strong sense that a part of a homily or a conference talk or a tape is meant specifically for them. Some will even hear a semi-audible voice as I did that morning after Mass in Cambridge. Some people "see" guidance; they will discern something from the Lord while reading scripture or spiritual books or Christian magazines or a letter from a friend.

Many people have recognized no particular pattern to the Lord's communication with them. Some typically go through a long period of uncertainty about whether a particular sense is from God. But everyone I have ever known who has seriously attempted to follow Christ has experienced guidance that is familiar in some sense. When the guidance is communicated in a way we have heard before, we can pursue it with great confidence. When it comes in a way that we haven't experienced before, we need to reflect on it more deeply. But in the end we will be comfortable with it. If not, if a communication from the Lord seems strange or deeply upsetting, we will need a considerable amount of confirming prayer and counsel before we accept it as valid.

> *Sammantha had splendid talent as a poet. She won a national poetry competition while still in high school and published two books of poems while a college undergraduate. Her creative writing teachers at the elite Ivy League school she attended said they could remember no young poet in their classes who was so talented. They urged her to pursue poetry as a career; she might achieve greatness, they said.*
>
> *Sammantha had other interests and talents too. She played the piano, sang in the choir, and was active in a program at the campus Catholic parish that tutored elementary school kids who were in scholastic trouble. She was pursuing a dual major in architecture and literature. For years, she had been thinking about a career in architecture.*
>
> *Sammantha's poetry teachers were very persua-*

sive, however. They advised her to pursue an academic career because most professional poets support themselves as college professors. Putting other possibilities aside without much thought, Sammantha went on to graduate school.

Problems cropped up. She discovered that she didn't particularly like teaching the freshman and sophomore classes she was assigned to as a teaching assistant. She was bored and annoyed by many of her graduate seminars. Discussion often focused on abstruse critical theories; seldom around the artistry and human significance of the text. The trouble became a crisis when she began research for her dissertation, a textual analysis of a minor Elizabethan poet. She disliked the research, resented the time it took and the tedium of the work. She fought a growing feeling that she wasn't suited for the life of a professor of literature.

But the feeling persisted, grew more intense, and finally became a clear conviction. Sammantha decided she had acted unwisely in entering graduate school. She hated her program. And the career it was preparing her for didn't appeal to her at all.

So she quit.

The consistency test must be applied carefully.

It's normal to examine our options in light of our God-given talents and abilities. A girl who enjoys math and solving complex number problems will look at careers in engineering or science. A successful salesman will naturally look for a job in sales or marketing when he decides it's time to move on. A big, strong kid might go out for the football team. A nurse who wants greater responsibilities would ordinarily look for further training in a medical field.

These are intuitive applications of the consistency test. Yet we must be careful. Our known abilities and past experiences do not determine our future roles and options. God is quite capable of surprises. He raises up the weak and small to confound the strong: Joseph over his brothers and Pharaoh; David over Goliath; Israel herself as a nation; an obscure carpenter's Son from Galilee over the kingdom of darkness. A fit between our skills and roles is important. But it doesn't have to be a perfect fit, and sometimes God calls us to act in a way that doesn't seem to fit our personal history at all.

Another pitfall of the consistency test is reversing the process. Instead of examining future possibilities in light of past accomplishments and abilities, we think that since a talent or interest already exists, the call to pursue it must be present as well. Sammantha made this mistake. She assumed (without thinking about it too carefully) that the presence of her great writing talent meant that she was called to make her career teaching literature and writing poetry. Perhaps, but not necessarily. It turned out that she wasn't suited for an academic career. Even if she *was* so suited, that in itself wasn't necessarily a sign that she was called to pursue it.

Consistency is just a test; it's not the call itself. Large decisions such as a career direction, the choice of a course of studies, a change of lifestyle or ministry commitments demand careful reflection and the weighing of many factors, one of which is the future's consistency with the past. We can expect the Lord to call us to use the talents He gave us. But our talents and interests don't constitute His call.

An emphasis on the wrong kind of consistency can waylay us in another way. We can find ourselves being consistent with the wrong things.

> *The phone call from Frank was the fourth emergency in as many months. He was about to be evicted from his apartment. Could Linda, his oldest sister, bail him out of a jam once again?*
>
> *Last month's emergency was literally bail — bail to get him out of jail on a drug possession*

charge. The month before that, his car had been wrecked and he had asked to borrow money to buy another. Before that, Linda had nursed Frank for a week while he recuperated from injuries suffered in a bar fight. Linda had done everything she could to help her brother. She felt called to do this out of loyalty to their dead parents, who had made the rehabilitation of the multi-troubled Frank a major project of their declining years. Frank wasn't being rehabilitated, and Linda could no longer cope with the stress of dealing with Frank, along with the guilt she felt at the thought of cutting him loose.

A Christian counselor helped Linda see that she was acting out of past guilt in her attitude about her brother. She was doing what her parents would have done, not what she could and should do. She was trying to repair damage inflicted in the past. She was being consistent with the past all right, but with patterns rooted in the past that should be changed.

Linda's predicament is quite common. We make commitments based on a sense of obligation or duty or responsibility that can sound eerily like a "call" from God but which should be critically reexamined instead. We should beware concluding that some new decision passes the consistency test simply because it continues us in a pattern of behavior that is rooted in the past.

Priests and religious are especially vulnerable to guilt. I have known many priests who have been drawn into demanding political commitments and social action projects by a feeling that they hadn't been doing enough to relieve poverty and injustice. Often they see their decision to get further involved in social action programs as simply a continuation of a commitment that had always been present in their ministries. Often, however, the social programs swallow them up. They find themselves involved in work that they do not have the skills to effectively perform. Frequently it also takes them away from their primary assignment of caring for people in a parish, teaching in a school, or serving in a hospital or retreat house.

Priests and religious are typically bombarded by demands on their time and are constantly exposed to people with serious needs. We receive many invitations to serve, more than we can possibly accept. In many cases, we are presented with situations where it can plausibly be said that if we don't help, no one will. Priests and religious need to always carefully discern how we spend our time and invest our energies. We are in obvious danger of making bad decisions about our work if we are afflicted with personal guilt about the condition of society.

Every need is not a call. This warning applies to everyone, not just people who work full time in the Church. When applying the consistency test, we need to look closely at the nature of the commitments and interests we have. Where are our first responsibilities? If we feel a strong emotional pull to take on added responsibilities or follow a major new course in our lives, where is that emotion coming from?

Are we being consistent with something that needs healing instead of heeding?

> *Paul runs a very successful mutual fund specializing in growth stocks. His job is simply described, very difficult to execute: buy stocks in good growing, profitable companies, preferably long before other investors discover them. In practice, Paul and his staff of analysts constantly make difficult judgments. Did this company have a sound plan? Were the top managers good enough to execute it? Did they have enough capital? Was the company strong enough to survive a recession? Paul made mistakes, but year after year his good choices were far more numerous than the bad ones.*
>
> *One evening at a family barbecue, Paul told his father one of the reasons for his success.*
>
> *"Sheila and Kent are my two best analysts. They*

*both have excellent analytical skills and good judg-
ment. Either of them is capable of sizing up the basic strengths and weaknesses of a company that we're
thinking about buying. But they are polar opposites
in temperament. Sheila is very cautious, skeptical,
always looking for problems, dubious about gran-
diose ideas. Kent is the optimist. He looks for the
companies others ignore: tiny firms with a great
product, companies coming out of bankruptcy in
good shape, inventors with a dream. He gets excited
easily. He finds winners no one else sees.*

*"We discuss possible new stocks to buy all the
time. I really pay attention when they react atypi-
cally — when Sheila gets excited over hidden possibilities in a stock that the rest of us haven't seen, or
Kent suddenly grows skeptical about a company that
looks pretty good to the rest of us. That's often a
warning to me. Sheila and Kent are very good when
applying their skills according to their temperament.
When they make judgments out of character, they're
often wrong."*

The consistency test calls on us to understand our temperament and emotional life. How do you ordinarily react to new
situations? Do you leap into them enthusiastically or are you
instinctively cautious, weighing every detail before deciding?
Is the prospect of change typically upsetting? Are you a dreamer,
prone to unrealistic hopes? Do you tend to be docile and trusting when people in authority ask you to do something? Include
your emotional make-up in the consistency test. Your reactions
to things provide important indications of the Lord's will for
you — especially when they are *inconsistent* with your usual
reactions.

A good example is an experience most of us have several
times in our lives — the chance to take on a new job. This is
always an important decision. You may be fearful; you find the

new responsibilities daunting and you doubt your ability to carry them out. In applying the consistency test, look at your emotional reactions in the past when you have been asked to do something new. If you typically feel a large dose of initial apprehension but go on to succeed in the new venture, you are probably on safe ground in not paying much attention to your anxiety. On the other hand, if you are someone who is typically energized by new challenges and experiences and you now feel doubt and foreboding, pay close attention. That may be a signal that the new idea is failing the consistency test.

Paul learned that the personalities of his stock analysts was an important factor in the normally unemotional world of financial analysis. Sheila's and Kent's judgment normally functioned most reliably within the framework of their normal temperaments. So it is with most of us — most of the time.

But not all the time. Sometimes God's will for us points in a direction contrary to the way our familiar emotional responses would lead us. Few of the martyrs for the faith thought in advance that they had the strength to endure suffering and death. But they accepted the Lord's invitation despite their doubt and fear. Similarly, we are sometimes called to a path that leads into the unknown.

The essence of our relationship with God is one of trust. He will care for us. He will give us the grace for the moment — not for all possible future moments. He gives the grace to begin our walk with him. We are to have trust that He will give us the grace for every circumstance — foreseen and unforeseen — along that path.

This is the most important application of the consistency test. It is more crucial to be consistently trusting in God's love and grace than in anything else.

Much of the decision-making I have done as president of Franciscan University has been marked by the need to trust God as He works out a plan over a period of years. When I first took the office, I made some important decisions about the direction of the college that turned out to be foundational for a succession of future decisions and initiatives. Some of these changes were huge, expensive, and risky. But since they were part of the working-out of a plan for renewal of the college already underway, deciding whether or not to undertake them was a relatively straightforward task.

When I became president of the College of Steubenville in 1974, the school was troubled on many fronts. Enrollment was declining, finances were precarious, students and staff were unhappy. The overarching need, I felt, was restoration of a fully Christian, Catholic, and Franciscan vision for the college. Where to start? I prayed specifically for an answer to that question.

I sensed a powerful direction to pay attention to the social and spiritual life of the students. Social life was coarse and barren; it largely revolved around alcohol and sex. Spiritual life was impoverished. Student life needed reform.

In prayer, I received the concept of "households" for students. These would be small groupings, overseen by an older advisor, where students would meet weekly for prayer, discussion, planning, and social activities. The idea of small groups for students was itself relatively non-controversial, and, in reality, not so unusual. What was sure to cause debate, however, was my proposal to make households mandatory. Yet I thought student life was the Lord's priority for the college and mandatory households the best way to address it.

My next step was to test the idea with a group of trusted colleagues. It would be a major initiative, a bold statement of where the school's leadership wanted to take the college, a step that was sure to be controversial, and might even be rejected by a significant portion of the student body. We examined the idea from every angle.

Would it be consistent with a Christian, Catholic, and Franciscan vision for the college?

Would it be a vehicle for the conversion of individual students? Would it positively affect the social and spiritual tone of the campus?

Could we do it? Were we willing to pay the price for such a

major change? Was mandatory student households really the issue for an investment of major energy from faculty, staff, and administrators at this time?

Were top administrators and staff sufficiently united about the proposal? Could we sell it to a skeptical audience?

We experimented with a few voluntary households and asked students to participate in the evaluation. And, of course, we continually held the idea up in prayer. Was this what *God* wanted?

I have told the story of households many times. We went ahead with them. We encountered some overt opposition and much passive-aggressive resistance. The faculty and staff moderators invested vast amounts of energy in making the households work. Some students never did come to like them, and the household requirement played a part in the decision of some students not to return to the college. But, overall, they were a tremendous success. The households broke through the anonymity and cynicism of student campus life. Most students welcomed the small group forum for discussion, socializing, and prayer. Quickly, the tone of the campus changed. The college was on its way to becoming an environment that was pleasant, constructive, and spiritually alive.

Many other changes at the college followed the pattern established here. In hindsight, I can see that at the time we applied a series of tests for decision-making that are, in essence, the tests presented in this book. This process became the model for future decision-making procedures, and the thinking behind households became a major part of the consistency test that we applied to subsequent proposals and initiatives.

Will this idea promote a Christian, Catholic, and Franciscan vision for higher education? Will it lead to conversion of heart and mind for those affected by it? Do we have the financial and human resources for it? What will we *not* be able to do if we do this? Is it consistent with what we've been doing?

What does *God* want?

After the household decision came many other initiatives.

These included the development of a program of summer conferences, a high quality theology major program, launching a pilgrimage office, inauguration of a Christian nursing bachelor's degree, a master's program in theology, an honor's program, a program in Catholic culture, and development of a series of courses and programs in life in the Holy Spirit and Christian growth and relationships.

A plan took form early on. The changes that followed were consistent with it.

The consistency test can lead you to ask five questions: Who? What? Where? When? How?

- *Who?* Does the Lord typically act through other people in your life — a spouse, spiritual director, close friends or family members, a cherished spiritual writer or speaker?
- *What?* Is your life with God following a pattern of a certain kind of work? Have you been acquiring skills and experience that point in a particular direction?
- *Where?* Do you hear God in certain places — in church, on long walks along a river, by the ocean, in your study?
- *When?* Do you feel guidance from God on an annual retreat, in silent prayer after communion, during Lent, or other times?
- *How?* Do you "hear" the Lord in personal prayer or through the words of others, "see" His word to you in scripture or in spiritual reading?

By carefully answering these questions, you should be able to see a pattern of His action in your life, a standard that can give you confidence that you are indeed discerning His will for you.

In working with students, I have developed another list of questions that many of them have found helpful. I call this exercise "Is it God?" The idea is to help them compare their inner sense of God's will with the revelation of God from established sources. I suggest that the students take some time to pray and then ask themselves these questions about their sense:

- Is it the God of scripture?
- Is it the God who has inspired my life in the past?
- Is it fitting and worthy of God?
- Is it the God who has spoken to me through other people in the past?

These questions highlight the core of the consistency test.

Another helpful question involves the cost of following a particular direction. Is the cost too high for what is being gained?

Of course God will not ask us to do anything sinful or immoral. But we sometimes find ourselves in a situation where pursuit of a lesser good will seriously undermine a higher good that God has already given us. Pursuit of a new business venture can exact too high a price from our care of our spouse and children. Volunteer activities can seriously distract us from fulfilling already settled commitments. New financial commitments need to be scrutinized with particular care. The cost may literally be too high.

We must be careful about this test. God can ask us to give away everything we have — even our lives — for Him. But we need to make sure a costly call is from Him and for Him.

My fellow Franciscan, St. Maximilian Kolbe, heard God's consistent call for his life in Auschwitz, the Nazi concentration camp in Poland. Maximilian had told his friends that their lives were divided into three parts: preparation, apostolate, and suffering. When the German arrests in Poland began, they were entering the third phase — suffering. He urged them to embrace suffering as willingly as they had the first two.

He followed his words with actions once he was a prisoner in Auschwitz. He gave of his meager food to others. He spent a portion of his hours of sleep making sure others were comforted. He forgave the guards and even heard their confessions.

Then ten prisoners were selected for death by starvation as punishment for an escape attempt. One of them, Francis Grazonigeck, cried out, "What will happen to my wife and children?" In that cry, Maximilian Kolbe heard a call from the Lord that was consistent with his past words on embracing suffering. He took the place of the anguished prisoner in the starvation bunker.

He was following the gospel injunction of Jesus, "Love one another. As I have loved you, so you also should love one another" (Jn 13:34) and "No one has greater love than this, to lay down one's life for one's friends" (Jn 15:13). John also writes, "The way we came to know love was that he laid down his life for us; so we ought to lay down our lives for our brothers" (1 Jn 3:16).

Summary
Is It Consistent?

1. What? Is it consistent with God's earlier calls in my life?

2. How? Is it consistent with how God has dealt with me in the past?

3. Who? Is it consistent with whom God has used in the past to lead me to His will?

4. When? Have I heard His call at the same time (or in the same way) that I have heard Him in the past? (Daily prayer time, after communion, on annual retreat, etc.)

5. Where? Have I heard His call in the same place or under the same circumstances that I have heard Him in the past? (In church, during a walk in the woods, in a special place of prayer, etc.)

6. How much? Is the cost, including possible negative effects, consistent with my established priority of values?

Conclusions about consistency

Chapter 4
What Confirms It?

Decision-making is a process. There often comes a moment — a meeting, a prayer time, a quiet weighing of pros and cons — when it can be said that we "make the decision." In reality, this moment of conviction follows the confirmation of a decision.

In making choices, we prayerfully examine whether a course of action will *conform* to God's revealed will and whether it draws us and others closer to *conversion* of our hearts. We consider its *consistency* with God's previous actions in our lives and whether the prompting to take a certain course is familiar to us. Once we formulate a tentative decision, it's very important to seek *confirmation* for it. We should do this as prayerfully and as carefully as any other part of the process of practical, Christian decision-making.

Usually, other people will be involved in our decisions in some form; we try out our ideas with them and listen to their views. Often circumstances will provide confirmation; doors will open, resources become available, possibilities turn into solid realities. Some decisions are confirmed after the fact as we see the fruit they bring — bad as well as good. Occasionally the Lord will confirm a decision through signs and wonders — a seemingly supernatural event or a miraculous manifestation of a natural occurrence. Confirmation sometimes comes before we make a final decision; sometimes it comes afterwards. Almost all decisions — save marriage and religious vocation — can be re-opened later.

When she turned forty, Kathi began to think seriously about working full time. Her two children

were in high school; college expenses loomed as demands on her time at home diminished. Her part-time job as a receptionist in a lawyer's office wasn't very exciting and it didn't bring in very much money. She thought of getting a full-time job in some other line of work. She also thought about going back to school.

Several of her friends thought she should get a new job right away. "You'd be great in real estate," said one. "Don't waste your time in school. It's expensive too."

But Walter, her husband, thought Kathi should seriously consider school. She would be happier with a professional job she was well prepared for, he thought. She might earn more in the long run. And, he thought, school could be financed with some of their savings and student loans. Kathi's sister Ann, her lifelong confidante, agreed.

What should she study? Kathi considered three possibilities: business, nursing, and social work. For three months she explored each field. She looked at degree programs, their costs, and the time each would take to complete. Could she get admitted? How good were the programs? What were local employment prospects in each field? How much could she earn? She talked to dozens of people in the course of this investigation.

She finally decided to try to get a master's degree in social work. That field didn't pay as much as the others, and sometimes jobs took longer to find. But Kathi thought she would be more satisfied in social work. Walter, Ann, and the priest who knew Kathi best all agreed.

We make our own decisions. But we almost never make decisions on our own. Input from others can take many forms.

Often, as in Kathi's case, we cannot even properly examine the options we have without involving many other people. Some decisions require the consent of others — a potential employer, a university admissions officer, the person you want to marry. In others, we should seek a degree of consensus about a decision from the people whose lives will be affected by it. Other decisions call for discussion and consultation instead of assent. In any case, it is almost always a good idea to seek input from other people before we make final decisions. The bigger the decision, the more important it is to consult broadly and extensively.

This simply makes good sense on a human, practical level. On our own, we overlook things. We can do our best to identify and weigh all the factors involved in a change in our lives, but we seldom can do this ourselves. Kathi knew little about degree requirements and job prospects in professional fields when she began to think about a job change. She had to gather and evaluate much information, and to do this she had to talk to many people. Administrators of large organizations — such as universities — are aware of the Law of Unintended Consequences. All large changes — no matter how carefully planned — have effects that no one foresees. A major goal of consultation with others is to anticipate and take into account as many of these consequences as possible.

Consultation and discussion can also counteract our natural, human tendency to deceive ourselves. We *want* the larger house, the more powerful computer, the master's degree, the beautiful woman, the charming, attentive man. We might be aware of the risks involved and the price to be paid in acquiring the desired object, but our natural tendency is to minimize the seriousness of these problems and overestimate our ability to deal with them. The stronger our desire, the stronger our inclination to talk ourselves into deciding that what we want is really the best thing to do.

Other people can help us counteract this human weakness — if we are wise and humble enough to ask them about it.

A final reason why we should involve others in our decision-making: We are communal creatures. We belong to families and communities. We are parts of networks of friends and colleagues and co-workers. We belong to the Church — a faith community that is the place where we live out our Christian lives. Today, in our secularized Western technological culture, our bonds to these communities are looser than they have ever been in human history. Personal autonomy and individual freedom are high cultural values. But autonomy flies in the face of our nature. When we make decisions, we should act within the web of obligations and relationships we live in.

Input from others can take many forms. The key factor is that the people you share your decisions with be people who know *you*. You should be in regular contact with them. They should be on the same spiritual wavelength. They should know you well enough to be aware of your strengths and weaknesses.

In Kathi's case, some of her acquaintances thought she should get a job selling real estate. Kathi might have succeeded at this work and made a lot of money, but it wouldn't have satisfied other desires. Her casual friends didn't know that. Her husband, sister, and spiritual director did.

We should look in the same places for good advice about our decisions. Spouses, spiritual directors, family members, and close friends tend to know us well.

A small group is another venue for discernment and confirmation. Many Catholics have been introduced to small groups though parish renewal programs and movements such as Cursillo and charismatic renewal. Groups are not for everyone, and it always takes time to build a level of openness and trust that is high enough for meaningful personal sharing. But they can be very valuable — even indispensable.

Since 1971, I have met every week with a group of Franciscan friars. The group has changed in membership over the years, but it has been an anchor in my life. My brothers in the group know *me*. They know my joys and sorrows. They have heard my life story in some detail. They know where I have succeeded and where I have failed. They know about my desires, my hopes, my sins, my temptations. I tell them about my prayer life. They monitor the condition of my soul.

I also bring all my important and difficult decisions to the group, along with any sense I have about what direction to go with them. When they confirm a direction, I feel empowered to go ahead and pursue it, and make whatever commitments it entails. The brothers take a personal concern for me. They tell me when I look tired and need to get away for a while. I do the same for them. This is the Church in action.

For priests and religious, this kind of small group is often the equivalent of the lay Catholic's family, which Vatican II calls "the domestic Church." But small groups are valuable for lay people as well; if at all possible, consider establishing or joining a group that is based on prayer and confidence in the Holy Spirit's guidance. It will take time and work, but group sharing and discernment can immeasurably increase your capacity to hear and follow the Lord.

I also bring every important decision affecting Franciscan University to the President's Team — a small group of top administrators that meets weekly for prayerful review of the school's major concerns. Many of us belong to organizations that have similar established structures for reviewing options and discerning decisions. Make use of them, when appropriate, for your own decision-making.

Keep several points in mind when you are seeking input from others.

The most valuable advice will come from people who know you well and share your faith commitments. You can get valuable information from other people, but rely most heavily on those who know you *personally.*

Keep in mind the degree of assent required from the people you consult. Friends — even close friends — should not think they have a veto over your career or schooling decisions. On the other hand, a woman you are interested in marrying *does* have a veto over your decision. A priest or other individual with pastoral authority over you must be heeded when he tells you that your proposed course of action violates God's law. Similarly, one spouse should ordinarily heed serious objections from the other over proposals to move the family, spend savings, quit a job, or other matters gravely affecting the whole family.

Finally, know when to stop talking. Endless consultation can be a problem. Too much input can paralyze action. There comes a point when everyone with a contribution to make has spoken, every peril (you hope) has been identified, all the pros and cons have been hashed out. The decision is yours. Make it.

Jill was strongly drawn to working with the poor. She wanted to spend part of her time during her last semester in college working as a volunteer in a twenty-four-hour crisis center in town. The problem was she had no time. She had to take a full load of classes in order to graduate and she worked a part-time waitress job to pay necessary expenses. Still, she took the training for the crisis center volunteers, even though she didn't think she would be able to actually become a volunteer.

One afternoon during the beginning of the winter semester, on an impulse, she asked her academic advisor whether there was any way she could receive academic credit for volunteer work at the crisis center. It had never been done before. Nevertheless, she submitted a written request.

Two days later, the chairman of the psychology department approved the idea. Jill could do the volunteer work, submit a research paper at the end of the semester, and receive the credit she needed to graduate.

•

Frank and Donna needed a larger house for their

family of six. They found a home that would suit their needs, but they couldn't make the numbers work. The bank was willing to approve the mortgage, but Frank and Donna were very uncomfortable with the size of the monthly payment. It would stretch their budget to the limit. Various "creative financing" alternatives suggested by their realtor and the bank's mortgage officer seemed fiscally imprudent. The house was slipping away.

Then Donna received a registered letter from a lawyer on the other side of the country. In it was a check made out to her for $9,000. Her grandmother, who had died the previous year, left that sum to each of her four grandchildren. Donna was stunned; she'd had no idea she was a beneficiary of her grandmother's estate.

Frank and Donna applied the money to their down payment. That reduced the monthly payment on the mortgage to a level they could handle comfortably. They bought the house.

•

Because Tom's job transfer had happened suddenly, he and Melanie got a late start on looking at schools in their new city. They decided to put their five-year-old daughter in a kindergarten at a Catholic school, but there were no openings in the class. Two days after their daughter started in a public school, the Catholic school principal called. An opening in the kindergarten had appeared; their daughter could enroll after all.

"Aren't we lucky!" Melanie exclaimed.

Our decisions are very often confirmed through the unfolding of favorable circumstances. Doors open and close. We run into key people unexpectedly. We hear about job openings in casual conversation with friends. The time and money to do something we feel the Lord wants us to do appear in unusual ways.

In fact, favorable circumstances are so common that we often attribute them to good luck. Like Melanie, we think we are simply fortunate when an obstacle disappears and we are able to do something we have been wanting to do. In reality, God is often sending us a message through the favorable circumstances of life. The concrete circumstances of daily life — encounters among people, the ordinary workings of institutions, commonplace decisions people make about how they spend their time and money — are God's field of action and His tools for work. When concrete circumstances change to make possible something we have been praying for, we should consider this a probable confirmation from God that the direction we have been pursuing is His will.

For example, I recall two men whom I met seemingly by chance at a time when I had been praying hard for financial help for Franciscan University.

One called my office and asked to see me on a day I had set aside for solitude and prayer. I felt a strong prompting to make an exception and see him — something I almost never did. He wanted to talk about sending one of his children to the university. I was able to help him with some personal needs. After that meeting, he dropped by often and we became friends.

I met the other man at a luncheon during my travels. I saw him standing in a buffet line and felt a prompting to meet him. I excused myself from the chat I was having, crossed the room, got into line behind him, and introduced myself. He smiled and said, "Father, I have a question. The gospel at Mass today directed us to 'pray always.' How is this possible?" This led to a conversation he found helpful. We also became good friends.

Both men eventually became substantial financial benefactors of Franciscan University. Their financial commitments came after we developed close personal relationships, during which I was aware of God's power at work in the circumstances in the lives of three busy men to draw us together.

An observer could look at these relationships and say that I was simply being a resourceful university president, cultivating relationships with two wealthy men who might eventually become benefactors. But I *knew* there was more to it than that. Our paths crossed at a time when I was fervently praying for financial help. The relationships developed more smoothly than one would have expected. I took this combination of circumstances as the Lord's confirmation of the direction I had embarked on.

Circumstances can *dis*confirm as well as confirm. If the needed time and money never materialize, if the college turns you down, if the girl says no to the date, if your ideal employer offers the job to someone else, you can take this as a sign to look for another direction.

More broadly, repeated circumstantial barriers can cause us to reexamine a decision that we had thought was guided by the Holy Spirit.

If you are turned down by six medical schools, you should reconsider your decision to become a doctor. If, after years of trying, you cannot find a university teaching job, you should prayerfully consider another line of work, despite your Ph.D. If the car breaks down, you may have to buy another one instead of taking that long-awaited family vacation.

Always look at circumstances with the eyes of faith. The fact is that there is always a plausible, non-spiritual explanation for the unfolding of favorable or unfavorable circumstances. Donna's inheritance check arrived at just the right moment, confirming their decision to buy a new house. But it was just a check in the mail which was coming in any event, sent by a lawyer who knew nothing of their financial need. Tom and Melanie's daughter got to go to the school they wanted, but it happened through a normal progression of circumstances. The natural appearance of these events can cause us to miss their spiritual significance.

Their significance comes from their context. If we are pursuing a certain direction prayerfully, if it's consistent with God's past dealings with us, then we can see the appearance of favorable circumstances and the disappearance of obstacles as signs of confirmation.

> *The first sign of serious trouble came when George arrived for his first day at his new job at Riverview Nursing Home: the new director of social services didn't have an office. "We're very short of space," his boss explained. "You can use a table in the dining room for paperwork until we can do something about it."*
>
> *Over the next three months, nothing was done about getting an office for George. Other serious problems piled up. Money that George had been promised for his program never materialized. The administrators of the nursing home constantly bickered with each other. The nursing staff appeared to be poorly trained and turnover was very high. Plans were made to address the home's problems, but they were never implemented. Specific promises to remedy certain immediate problems were broken. In an atmosphere of constant crisis, George found himself working many nights and most weekends. He was under constant pressure. Patient care was substandard. Staff relationships were poisoned by rivalries and savage office politics.*
>
> *After many conversations with the director and other administrators, George decided that nothing was going to change at Riverview. He concluded that his decision to take this job had been mistaken — or, at least, whatever good that was going to come from it had already come. He began to look for another job. When he found one, he gave notice.*

Galatians 5:22-23 is one of the most familiar passages in the letters of Paul: "The fruit of the Spirit is love, joy, peace, patience, kindness, generosity, faithfulness, gentleness, self-control." It is also one of the most useful in seeking confirmation for our decisions. The assurance we need that our direction is the right one often comes through an assessment of its "fruit." Some are marks of our inner state of mind: love, joy, and peace. Some can be observed outwardly in relationships: kindness, generosity, and faithfulness. Paul contrasts the fruit of the Spirit with the works of the flesh, many of which are plainly visible: hatreds, rivalry, jealousy, outbursts of fury, acts of selfishness, dissensions, factions, occasions of envy (Gal 5:20-21). When these are present, we have a clear indication that we should not make a proposed decision or, if it is made, that it should be reconsidered.

The fruit of the Spirit was important for me in my own decision in 1957 to enter the Franciscans. I had known for more than a year that God wanted me to be a priest. But I didn't know what kind of priest. I considered the diocesan priesthood and several religious orders. It was a difficult time of stress and hesitation. I told few people about my vocation; I did not tell my own family.

When I visited the Franciscans in Loretto, Pennsylvania, I knew my search was over. I felt as if I had come home. After deciding to seek admission to the Third Order Franciscans, I immediately experienced the inner fruit of the Spirit that Paul writes about. A sense of joy surged through me. I felt a peace that was far deeper and more profound than simple relief at having finally settled on a direction for my life. My decision was also confirmed by the religious superiors of the Franciscan order, who also discerned a vocation in me and admitted me to the seminary.

It was not, of course, a final decision. That would come with ordination after years of preparation and discernment, involving many other people in the centuries-old manner of entry into the religious life.

My family, however, did not manifest the fruit of the Spirit when I told them about my plans. I am an only child. My mother was grief-stricken at the news that she would never have grand-children. My father, who had been divorced from my mother for many years, thought I had been brainwashed by religious fanatics. He thought I would be wasting my talents and a Harvard law degree. My mother's husband was furious at me for "breaking your mother's heart."

Nevertheless, I went ahead and entered the seminary. Family reactions to major life decisions should ordinarily be carefully considered. But the call from God to be a priest had been clear, strong, and consistent. It had been confirmed in many ways. And there was plenty of time to test it before it was irrevocable.

Over the next seven years, the fruit of the Spirit transformed the lives of my three closest family members. My mother and father both returned to the sacramental life of the Church and died as faithful Catholics. My mother experienced an exceptional transformation; she spent her last years in the practice of habitual contemplative prayer. My stepfather, who had never been a Christian, converted and embraced the Catholic Church.

The manifestation of the fruit of the Spirit in my family played no direct part in confirming my vocation. My own continuing experience of the fruit of the Spirit — love, joy, peace, self-control, and the rest — throughout seminary and beyond did play an important part in confirming it. But my family's change played an indirect role. It was another sign that I was on the right course. For them, my shocking and disappointing decision became a source of grace in their own lives, an occasion to hear the Lord's invitation to love and serve Him. I praise and thank Him for it.

We should look for the fruit of the Spirit at the time of decision. If you are restless, uneasy, unsure, or confused when the time comes to make up your mind, pause and reflect. Ask the Lord specifically to resolve the turmoil if the proposed direction is really His will. Consult again with a spiritual director, close friend, or other person who knows you well and shares your faith commitment.

Look for the fruit of the Spirit as you proceed down the path that you have chosen. I found it in the seminary. George did not find it in his job at Riverview Nursing Home. There is no formula for measuring fruits of the Spirit. But we should look for them and take their presence or absence as signs of confirmation.

The Lord does not give us grace for our lives before we live them. He promises sufficient grace, not perpetual assurance. Often we will not experience love, joy, peace, patience, kindness, generosity, faithfulness, gentleness, self-control until we act. But when we set forth on a course guided by the Holy Spirit, we can expect His fruit to be there.

Miraculous signs and wonders are the final source of confirmation. These include overtly supernatural phenomena such as visions, locutions, dreams, and healings, as well as conjunctions of natural events that are so improbable that they seem to require a supernatural explanation.

The Bible contains many examples of directions given or confirmed by signs and wonders. Jesus' miracles confirmed His authority, proclaimed the gospel, and announced the kingdom of God. Mary and Joseph are warned away from Herod in a dream. Peter's dream tells him that the gospel is to be preached to Gentiles too. God sends seven plagues to send a message to Pharaoh. He speaks to Moses from a burning bush.

Many saints have experienced confirming signs through visions and locutions. They include Catherine of Siena, Teresa of Avila, Francis of Assisi, Anthony of Padua, Joan of Arc, and Padre Pio. People in our own day have experienced them as well.

Signs and wonders raise complicated issues of discernment. I cannot discuss them thoroughly here; I want to make only a few simple points.

There is little point in looking for signs and wonders; in

fact, we run risks of deluding ourselves if we seek them. By definition they are miraculous. They operate outside natural laws. By definition they are rare. If they were commonplace, they wouldn't be wonders. It's enough to know that they sometimes happen and that God can use them to confirm us in the path He wishes us to follow.

When they do happen, the basic task of discernment is to determine whether the phenomenon is from God and, if so, to what purpose. This is the responsibility, first of all, of the person receiving the sign and also of anyone consulted to help discern it.

Be careful about signs and wonders. The spiritual realm is populated by evil spirits too. While they cannot do permanent harm to God's faithful sons and daughters, they can sow confusion through false signs. Always be slow to conclude that you are in fact experiencing a supernatural sign, and don't make a major decision on the basis of a miraculous sign that you haven't discussed with anyone else.

Summary

What Confirms It?

1. Is it confirmed by those who are involved in the proposal?

2. Is it confirmed by apparent miraculous or spiritual signs?

3. Is it confirmed by people who know me and are in a position to give godly direction to me?

4. Is it confirmed by circumstances — either extraordinary or which make the decision possible?

5. Are there other signs that seem to confirm or deny the validity of the proposition as from God?

Conclusions about confirmation

Chapter 5
Conviction: Does the Heart Say 'Yes'?

For a year, Jack and Angela had been talking, thinking, and praying about adopting a child. They had been unable to conceive after five years of marriage, three of them in treatment for infertility. The doctors said they might eventually succeed, but possibly not. They had looked at adoption from every angle. The signs seemed to point toward going ahead.

Both had a strong desire to have children.

· *Having children certainly seemed to conform to their understanding of marriage.*

Their parents, close friends, and others they consulted confirmed the idea of adoption.

They had good jobs, a home of their own, even some savings. They were more comfortable financially than most young couples. Angela would be a full-time mother.

A social worker at an adoption agency thought their application would be approved and that they would eventually find a child to adopt.

There were risks, of course. Several well-publicized problem adoptions made Jack and Angela uneasy, and relationships in adoptive families could be difficult to manage as the years went by. The agency couldn't guarantee that they would find a suitable child. They worried that their reasons for wanting to adopt were selfish ones. They preferred to have natural children, something they might yet be able to do.

Conviction: Does the Heart Say 'Yes'?

Yet adoption seemed like a good course. It passed all the tests of discernment.

But Jack and Angela hesitated — for month after month. They talked and talked, prayed and prayed. They wrote down the reasons for and against adoption; the pros vastly outweighed the cons. Their minds were made up; it made perfect sense to go ahead. Yet their hearts were paralyzed. Something didn't "feel" right.

The final test of a decision is the inner conviction that this course of action is indeed the right one. Does the heart grasp it? Is there a sense of moral certainty that this direction is God's will? The first four tests emphasize the making up of the mind. Does the proposed direction conform to God's law? Does it bring us and others closer to Him? Is it consistent with the way the Lord has worked in our lives in the past? Is it confirmed by the counsel of others, by favorable circumstances, and by the fruit of the Spirit? Conviction is the test of the heart. Do we "know" inside that this is the right way?

It is not unusual to go through a lengthy process of discernment, feel convinced that a decision is the right one, and still be plagued by anxiety and fear. The bigger the decision, the less likely we are to reach the point of resolution in a state of perfect calm. Often — perhaps most of the time — uneasiness is a familiar, instinctive reaction to change. We can go ahead despite it — as long we have a sense of inner conviction beneath the surface turmoil.

But sometimes this conviction is not present. The mind is made up; the heart hesitates. The will is frozen.

I have counseled many people in this condition of "decision gridlock." I often try to unblock the heart by leading them to examine past decisions that they believe were led by God or were right in the sight of God. We pay special attention to the difference between peace in the heart and conclusion of the mind. The two should both be present in a major decision, but they are not the same thing. We focus on assessing the condition of the heart. Does the heart feel the same way now as it did when you made decisions that you believe were right? If not, what is the quality of the difference?

Often I suggest that the person ask the Lord two questions. "Lord, is it your will that I do this?" And then, "Lord, is it your will that I *not* do this?" By comparing the internal responses to these two questions, the person often finds the answer.

Gentle questioning like this can give focus to one's prayer. We often talk too much in prayer and don't listen. But when we try to listen, we can be plagued by distractions and unfocused silence. Putting a question to the Lord can break us through the fog of paralysis and uncertainty and allow our heart to open up to the will of God.

A conviction in the heart was missing when I was deciding whether to accept the job of president of the College of Steubenville in 1974. And gentle questioning in prayer helped me find it.

When the presidency question came up, I was quite happy in my job as rector of the T.O.R. seminary in Loretto, Pennsylvania. My superior asked me to interview for the opening, but without a sign that he thought this was the direction for me. "I need some qualified candidates to at least interview," he said.

I agreed to be interviewed. I knew that the final decision would be left to me if I was selected. Then I began testing the possibilities.

I sensed God saying to me, "What if I want you to be president of the College of Steubenville?" Perhaps this meant that God was asking me to reaffirm my vow of obedience to Him to go anywhere at any time, but He was not actually calling me to the presidency. Or perhaps he wanted me to be president of the college some time, but not now, when things were going so well at the seminary. Or another thought: maybe the Lord just wanted me to give my opinions in the interview and leave it at that. I played with all these ideas. I discussed them with my closest associates. I prayed about them.

I interviewed, gave my views on what the college needed, and was soon informed that I was the first choice for the job. Now there was a real decision to make, not just a possibility. It was suddenly very serious.

I followed the procedure I present here in this book. I consulted my brothers in my small fraternal group. I sought direction from my confessor. I weighed the pros and cons. There were many good reasons for staying as rector of the seminary, and some of my closest friends favored that. There were also good reasons to accept the presidency of the college. It passed the tests of conformity, conversion, and consistency and it was confirmed in several ways. It seemed like the right step.

Yet I could not resolve the matter in my heart. Conviction was lacking. The decision was mine. The reasons for going ahead seemed compelling, but they were on the order of intellectual analysis. The sense of inner peace at the prospect simply wasn't there. I began to question the Lord in prayer: Is it your will that I do this? Is it your will that I *not* do this?

As I struggled with my decision, I attended a conference where a speaker talked about his own struggles to give his life fully to God. He had always been afraid to surrender completely to the Lord's will, he said, because he feared that the Lord would send him into the jungles of Africa — and that terrified him. He had no desire whatsoever to be a missionary in Africa or any other place. So he withheld part of himself.

"Finally," the speaker said, "I did make a full commitment to the Lord despite my fears. And He didn't send me to Africa. I learned something — God never sends anyone to Africa without first putting Africa in his heart."

I was thunderstruck. I took these words as something that the Holy Spirit was directing to me in my own situation. *God never sends anyone to Africa without first putting Africa in his heart.* Do you want to put the College of Steubenville in my heart, Lord? I asked. As the speaker went on with his talk, as I sat on the stage behind him, I opened my heart in response to the invitation of the Spirit. I found the College of Steubenville already there. The conviction that this was the right direction settled on me. It has never left.

Conviction often takes time. In 1962, the future Pope John Paul II told a group of seminarians about his decision to become a priest. The young Karol Wojtyla was a manual laborer in a quarry near Krakow during the Nazi occupation of Poland. His father had died. He spent his spare time writing poetry and plays and acting in a theater troupe.

"During that period," he told the seminarians, "sparks were awakened in me concerning the most important problems in my life and the road of my vocation was decided ... I gradually became aware of my true path. I was working at a plant and devoting myself, as far as the terrors of the occupation allowed, to my taste for literature and drama. My priestly vocation took shape in the midst of all that, like an inner fact of unquestionable and absolute clarity."

If conviction does not come despite all our careful testing and prayer, we should not press it. There are degrees of conviction. We may obtain complete inner certainty that the proposed course is correct. However, conviction doesn't mean certainty. We may not be certain, but rather be sure enough about the decision to go ahead with it and trust God. If we follow the procedure of prayerful testing and deliberation outlined in this book, the chances are we will not make a decision that is displeasing to God even if we wish we had a stronger inner conviction.

On the other hand, it may well be the case that the matter is not ready for resolution. Delay may indeed be the proper course. The absence of conviction might be a signal to seek additional counsel or spiritual direction. Not to act — or not to act *now* — should be a decision in itself, not simply procrastination or paralysis.

I will discuss some of these problems in more detail in the next chapter.

Be reassured by the words of St. Francis de Sales:

> We must proceed in good faith and ... do freely what seems good to us, so as not to weary our minds, waste our time, and put ourselves in danger of disquiet, scruples and superstitions.

Summary

Does the Heart Say 'Yes'?

1. Do I have moral certainty about the proposal?

2. Can I say that I believe in my heart that this is the right thing to do?

3. Of my alternatives, of which I must choose one, is this the one I believe is right?

4. Am I convinced that this is simply a good thing to do without any appreciable negative consequences following?

5. Am I paralyzed with difficulties or uncertainties and therefore have to appeal to other principles or to guidance from others?

Conclusions about conviction

Chapter 6
Handling Difficulties

When he was president, Ronald Reagan was often accused of proposing simple answers to complex problems. He didn't deny it, but had a cheerful response.

"Just because it's simple doesn't mean it's easy," he would say.

This is a lesson Mr. Reagan learned time and again as president. It's something all of us are bound to learn sooner or later as we set about the task of discerning God's will for us as we set the course for our lives.

There's nothing complex about the basic framework for decision-making outlined in this book. So far I have emphasized its simplicity. We ask if a decision conforms to God's law. We look at its contribution to our ongoing conversion. We examine its consistency with our past life and previous commitments. We seek to confirm it through friends, circumstances, and the fruit of the Spirit. Before acting, we look for a sense of inner conviction in our hearts. Conformity, conversion, consistency, confirmation, and conviction. These five "Cs" are a practical method which can be applied to almost all the decisions we make, large or small.

But that doesn't mean it's easy. Frequently we feel there's a sixth "C" to contend with — confusion. Difficulties are a reality when making decisions. Here we will look at some of the more common ones.

Enthusiasm followed by unrest in your spirit. Everyone is thrilled when your son is invited to spend the summer working in a congressman's office in Washington. It's an honor, the position fits in well with his career plans, the work will be exciting. But it turns out that your son will have to work as a volunteer and pay his own expenses. He had planned to earn much of his college tuition with summer work. He could borrow the money — on top of his already heavy borrowing for college. He asks your advice. You are very uneasy.

When a good plan is accompanied by deep anxiety and you lack an inner conviction that this is the right thing to do, it's best not to act. The reasons for going ahead may be compelling and attractive. Your family and friends might be vigorously cheering you on. The advantages might be readily apparent, well worth the risks. But if an intense caution persists, be very reluctant to forge ahead.

Anxiety and sadness followed by an inner peace. You don't think your elderly mother should continue to live alone. Hiring a live-in companion or having her live with you or your sister are not desirable or practical solutions. The idea of moving her to a nursing home is very upsetting to your mother and everyone else in the family. You _could_ provide some temporary support for her, but that would be no answer. As you move toward a decision, your sadness about removing your mother from her home grows deeper, but an inner conviction that this is the right decision intensifies as well.

Some decisions are quite painful. They involve choosing the least unattractive of a number of unattractive options. Some decisions in life — including some of the most important ones — are thrust upon us against our will. Circumstances require that we act in situations we would rather not be involved in. Sometimes we must act in ways that bring pain to ourselves and others.

The emotional turmoil involved in difficult decisions can be a factor in decision-making, but it can also be an impediment to discerning the proper course. The key is to apply the tests of decision-making as objectively as possible and look for the sense of inner conviction that is our final signal to act. Even if our sadness never disappears, we can proceed if the conviction in our spirit is present.

Uncertainty about the conversion test. You've been asked to become chairman of your parish council. You are thinking about switching your college major from marketing to nursing. You have a feeling that you should donate most of some unexpected extra income to a local crisis pregnancy center.

An idea seems to pass all the tests except one: you are not sure whether it will bring you closer to God. Is it really part of His plan for the ongoing conversion of your life? Does it address a weakness of yours? Does it mobilize your talents for the work of the Kingdom? Will it force you into greater dependence on the Lord? Or will another plan accomplish these things more effectively?

When the remaining uncertainty involves conversion of the heart, it's usually best to give the Lord the benefit of the doubt. When it comes to conversion, He knows best. His purposes for our life are only partly known to us. If everything else about the decision lines up, we can safely act, trusting the Lord to take care of our conversion.

Conflicting signs. The most common difficulty in decision-making is dealing with conflicting signals. Some signs are positive; others are negative.

A job offer comes your way. You didn't seek it. The company, the responsibility, and the money all look very good. Your prayerful reflection on the idea yields positive senses. Yet when you ask your family and friends to confirm it, no one does. Some oppose it. Some have a vague unease about it.

You need a new car. A co-worker offers you a good deal on a car you like. You have the money for it. Your friends think it's a great idea. But you have to make a quick decision. You have never made a major purchase in your life without shopping carefully and deliberating long and hard. You're uncomfortable going ahead.

After long discussion and prayer, you and your husband decide not to build a lakeside home where you can vacation and eventually retire. However, a few months after your decision, changes in the real estate market make the second home more financially feasible. At the same time, a close friend of yours says she has a special revelation from God that you should proceed.

Decisions like these, where the various signs seem to be pointing in opposite directions, can be quite difficult to sort out.

Often, the best course is to take more time to pray about, reflect on, and discuss the issue. If taking more time means that the opportunity will pass, so be it. It's usually best not to make a decision under the pressure of circumstances. At the same time, realize that a choice not to act is also a decision.

If you hesitate simply because you are startled by the way an opportunity has come to you or because it involves something brand new in your life, your reluctance may prevent you from seeing something the Lord wants for you.

If the problem comes down to a difference between your perception and those of others, you should ordinarily follow your own convictions. God may use other people to make His will known to you, but He doesn't have to. You are responsible for your own actions — and inactions. You have no assurance that He will give anyone else the same insight into a decision that He gives you. And He surely doesn't give anyone else the responsibility to make your decisions.

No clear sign. Sometimes we will put a proposal through this process of testing and come out with no clear answer. You have two choices and each seems to pass the tests of conformity, conversion, and consistency. No confirming signs impress you. You have no spiritual sense about either choice. Both seem equally right.

This does not present a serious difficulty when the decision is of small consequence. You might agonize over whether to order pearl gray or metallic blue paint for your new car, but the choice has little impact on the welfare of your family or the work of the kingdom of God. Simply make the best choice based on the information you have.

There is a difficulty, however, when you perceive no clear sign about a decision that seems to call out for one. Which of these three candidates should you hire for a key position in your business? If you are a leader in a Christian organization, should you commit the organization to a close relationship with another group? Decisions like these have tremendous consequences for the future of the enterprise, for people for whom you are responsible, and for you personally. It is disconcerting, to say the least, when the Lord seems to have nothing to say about them.

The problem often lies within us. Our vision may be clouded. We may have a superficial notion about how the Lord works in our lives. We may have made a poor choice a while ago and are now experiencing the consequences. Our prayer lives might be in a period of dryness. We may be young — in years or in the Christian life or both. We don't have enough experience of God working in our lives to provide a good context for testing a decision. The Lord might be speaking; for whatever reason, we're unable to hear him.

I have been in this situation many times. I have usually concluded that the reason is because I have built my castle on the sand of wishful thinking, self-delusion, dreams, or any number of things that are less solid than God's word. I have often acted according to my best judgment at the time without a clear sense of the Lord's direction. Sometimes my choices have had positive results. Sometimes they have been failures. Usually my bad decisions have had good initial results but poor long-term effects. It is easier to see the immediate benefits of a new relationship or commitment and only later experience the burdens. Unfortunately, when you are relying on your own judgment, you tend to decide according to what you can easily see.

All of this leads to a vital point: you are not perfectly holy. Consequently, you are going to make poor choices and bad decisions. These should become fewer as you mature as a Christian and gain experience in the spiritual elements of discernment and decision-making. Poor choices and their consequences can always be an occasion to learn more about your weaknesses and they can create situations where you are forced to rely more on the Lord. Jesus is Lord over our mistakes as well as our successes.

Indecision about acting at all. We can sometimes address indecision by opening our hearts and perhaps gently questioning God, as I discussed in the last chapter. But sometimes God is calling you to go deeper in your life with Him.

In my avocation as a fisherman, I have often been told by experts that I must cast my line close to the bottom of the sea to get the big fish. The advice recalls Jesus' words to Peter to cast deeper into the Sea of Galilee. Sometimes God lets us experience being adrift in our lives so that He will catch our attention. He is calling us to a deeper life with Him through prayer, spiritual reading, the sacraments, fasting, vigils, retreats, or simply quieting down and listening to Him. When we go deeper with Him, we can hear Him better.

St. Ignatius Loyola offered a biblical principle that can help us with indecision. He suggests that we imagine ourselves at the point of death, and standing before Jesus Christ at the final judgment. Looking back, which alternative course of action would we be most happy to have chosen? St. Ignatius urges us to practice what we would, in fact, say about our choice.

Indecision about an important step might be a call to lay a new spiritual foundation in your life. You may want to seek spiritual direction from a spiritual architect who can look at the whole structure and help you plan a renovation.

Approach difficulties in decision-making with confidence. They are opportunities to come to know the Lord better.

Chapter 7
Courage: A Vital Virtue

You will never make a decision that you are absolutely sure about. The only certainty is God's love. Every decision we make to respond to His love, every step we take on the path of faithfulness, every choice we make to fulfill the responsibilities He has entrusted to us carries an element of risk. Despite everything, we might be wrong. Blessed John Henry Newman, the great nineteenth-century British churchman, spoke perceptively about how a moral certainty to go ahead can coexist with awareness that there's a risk of failure:

> Our duty as Christians lies in making ventures for eternal life without the absolute certainty of success ... This indeed, is the very meaning of the word 'venture'; for that is a strange venture which has nothing in it of fear, risk, danger, anxiety, uncertainty. Yes, so it certainly is; and in this consists the excellence and nobleness of faith, this is the very reason why faith is singled out from other graces, and honored as the especial means of our justification, because its presence implies that we have the heart to make a venture.

It takes courage to venture in faith. Courage is not a virtue separate from the rest. It is the *way* we develop every virtue. As C.S. Lewis said, "Courage is not merely one of the virtues, but the form of every virtue, precisely at its testing point, which is the highest point of reality."

Every virtue reaches its testing point. As we grow in love, we are eventually called to love the unlovable. As we grow in faith, we reach a point where we must believe when there is no apparent evidence. The virtue of hope grows in us until the time when everything is dark, when circumstances are impossible, when the thought of despair tempts us. We go along steadily in loyalty and faithfulness until the venture collapses, others abandon the work, and point the finger of blame at you.

Courage will carry us beyond these limits to virtue. The word "courage" means "to act with the heart." It comes from the deepest recesses of our spirits, the inmost being, the place where the self is grounded. Jesus is there. "In the world you will have trouble," He said, "but take courage, I have conquered the world" (Jn 16:33).

Frequently we must draw on our resources of courage to act rightly. Since decision and action always entail risk, it's not uncommon to experience fear and timidity when decision time comes, even if thorough testing of the alternatives has convinced us of the right course. We can venture forth in faith, stepping out with courage, knowing that God's grace is sufficient and that God will provide sufficient grace.

When our resources of courage are depleted, we need *en-*couragement — the infusion of courage. This comes from the Holy Spirit: The Church "was being built up and walked in the fear of the Lord, and with the consolation of the holy Spirit it grew in numbers" (Acts 9:31). It comes from scripture: "For whatever was written previously was written for our instruction, that by endurance and by the encouragement of the scriptures we might have hope" (Rom 15:4). Encouragement comes from each other: "Therefore, encourage one another and build one another up, as indeed you do" (1 Thes 5:11). Encouragement comes from God. Paul prays: "Blessed be the God and Father of our Lord Jesus Christ, the Father of compassion and God of all encouragement, who encourages us in our every affliction, so that we may be able to encourage those who are in any affliction with the encouragement with which we ourselves are encouraged by God" (2 Cor 1:3-4).

Pope John Paul II speaks often of courage. He made a particularly memorable exhortation at World Youth Day in

Denver in 1993: "Have the courage to commit yourself to the truth. Have the courage to believe the good news.... Take courage in the face of life's difficulties and injustices."

Peter, the first pope, showed courage — and the lack of courage — when Jesus called him to step out of the boat and walk to him on the water of the Sea of Galilee. Peter had no doubts. He knew it was Jesus on the water. He knew Jesus called him. He knew Jesus controlled the wind and the waves and would hold Peter up. We often find ourselves in the same position when making difficult decisions. We know the right choice. We know the Lord's will. We have confidence in God's grace. Yet, like Peter, we must still step out of the boat.

That takes courage. Peter had it — initially. He stepped out onto the water and began to walk toward Jesus, but then fear took hold again as he saw where he was in the midst of the wind and the waves. He began to sink. Jesus saved him and admonished him for his lack of faith. Like Peter, we step out in courage when we venture forth in obedience to the Lord. We sustain courage through faith.

If our faith falters, *when* it falters, Jesus will lift us up.

In the sixteenth century, the sculptor Donatello arranged to buy a two-ton block of marble for one of his works. When the dealer brought the block to Donatello's studio in Rome, the sculptor rejected it. He saw flaws in the stone. The dealer then took the marble to Michelangelo, hoping the artist would buy it and spare him the task of returning the block to the quarry. Michelangelo saw the flaws, but saw something else as well — a figure buried deep in the stone that he wanted to bring into existence. He bought the marble and created the statue of David, the world famous masterpiece now in a museum in Florence. Michelangelo used the flaws in the stone to portray some of the muscles in David's body.

Michelangelo said that he saw the figure of David buried in the stone. All he, the artist, had to do was cut away the stone on the outside and set David free.

Similarly, God sees the greatness within us; he wants to cut away the outside stone and set us free. He sees the flaws. Some he will remove; some he will use, as Michelangelo used the flaws in David's marble. Our flaws are part of His plan to bring forth holiness in us. He calls; we answer. By responding to His call with courage and faith, we can become saints.

Consider some of the many examples of courage in the scriptures.

David had to face a much larger and stronger enemy in man-to-man combat. Gideon was told to take on a vastly superior force with a small band of warriors. Abraham had to move his entire clan to a new country. Later he had to be willing to sacrifice his son. Moses had to confront the mighty Pharaoh. Then he had to step into the Red Sea.

All of these men trusted in the Lord. They walked in faith, stood on faith, moved forward in faith. Their stories are preserved in scripture in part to give us models of faith for our own walk.

Consider the courage of great saints like Thomas More and Isaac Jogues. St. Thomas could have avoided execution by making a simple act of submission to King Henry — a submission that high officials such as himself were accustomed to making. But Thomas's conscience forbade it and he went to his death proclaiming that he died as "the King's loyal subject but God's first."

Isaac Jogues had been brutally tortured and mutilated by the Mohawk Indians before being rescued by the intervention of the Dutch. Back in France, he turned down a comfortable position in a retreat house and elected to return to North America as a missionary to the Indians. He returned to the Mohawks; this time they killed him, as Isaac knew they might. Indeed, Isaac Jogues had prayed for the courage to become a martyr.

Courage of this kind calls for prayer. In his book *Crossing the Threshold of Hope*, Pope John Paul II suggests that we meditate at length on this passage from Romans, "in order to understand profoundly the meaning of prayer":

> For creation awaits with eager expectation
> the revelation of the children of God; for
> creation was made subject to futility, not
> of its own accord but because of the one
> who subjected it, in hope that creation it-
> self would be set free from slavery to cor-
> ruption and share in the glorious freedom
> of the children of God. We know that all
> creation is groaning in labor pains even
> until now; and not only that, but we our-
> selves, who have the firstfruits of the Spirit,
> we also groan within ourselves as we wait
> for adoption, the redemption of our bod-
> ies. For in hope we were saved (Rom 8:19-
> 24).

The Holy Father quotes another verse: "The Spirit too comes
to the aid of our weakness; for we do not know how to pray as
we ought, but the Spirit himself intercedes with inexpressible
groanings" (Rom. 8:26). John Paul comments: "We begin to
pray, believing that it is our own initiative that compels us to do
so. Instead, we learn that it is always God's initiative within
us.... We must pray with 'inexpressible groaning' in order to
enter into rhythm with the Spirit's own entreaties."

God initiates our plans and is the driving force within them.
As we proceed with our decision-making, we must constantly
turn to Him in prayer, begging the Holy Spirit to come forth
and make new creations of us, to continue and complete the
work of transforming us into God's adopted sons and daughters. This may take much prayer — extended intercession. In a
sense, it is prayer that never stops, for the transformation of our
selves is work that is never finished.

Chapter 8
Making a Decision for Life

The biggest decisions are those that involve life-long vocations. These are, primarily, marriage and religious vocations to serve God as a priest, sister, or religious brother. In many cases, a call to live singly is also a life commitment that follows the same kind of intense discernment as other vocations.

Discerning a call to one of these vocations provides a special challenge to decision-making. They are calls to a permanent state in life. They can be examined carefully beforehand; some kinds of religious life can even be lived temporarily without committing oneself to them. But neither marriage nor the religious life can be "tried out." Neither can be discarded once entered into. They are the biggest of major decisions.

The word vocation means "call," but the English word "call" is too weak to capture the full meaning of the word. The vocation call is more like the biblical naming, as in Adam's naming the animals in the garden. There's something definitive about it. When God calls you to a vocation, he defines you for life. He possesses you, exerts His authority over you.

At the same time, a vocation is a call to freedom. It doesn't remove your free will. To the contrary, it enables you to become free. Many people see a vocation as something limiting — locking oneself up in a seminary or convent, or restricted for life by marriage vows to one partner. But it is not limiting at all. A vocation is a call to freedom, a response to the deepest desires of one's heart.

Our spirits are oppressed when we fight a call from God. When we have a vocation, the freedom comes in following it. "When the Son frees you, you are free indeed" (Jn 8:36).

The story of the rich young man in Matthew is often used as a model for discussion of religious vocations. However, it can be applied to discernment of *all* vocations — to the married and single life as well. This encounter between Jesus and the young seeker raises most of the important issues in the discernment of vocation. It's a very familiar passage, but read it carefully again:

Now someone approached him and said, "Teacher, what good must I do to gain eternal life?"

He answered him, "Why do you ask me about the good? There is only One who is good. If you wish to enter into life, keep the commandments."

He asked him, "Which ones?" And Jesus replied, "'You shall not kill; you shall not commit adultery; you shall not steal; you shall not bear false witness; honor your father and your mother'; and 'you shall love your neighbor as yourself.' "

The young man said to him, "All of these I have observed. What do I still lack?"

Jesus said to him, "If you wish to be perfect, go, sell what you have and give to the poor, and you will have treasure in heaven. Then come, follow me."

When the young man heard this statement, he went away sad, for he had many possessions.

Then Jesus said to his disciples, "Amen, I say to you, it will be hard for one who is rich to enter the kingdom of heaven" (Mt 19:16-23).

The young man is looking for a bargain: "What good must I do to gain eternal life?" Eternal life is a great prize; tell me what to do to gain it and I'll do it.

Jesus answers, as he always does, by drawing the questioner deeper into the mystery of God. The "good" you are talking about is the means to the end. It isn't really what you are after. "There is only one who is good," he points out. And that is God Himself.

Jesus then moves on to the means to this end: keep the commandments. The young man, still bargaining, asks, "Which ones?" Jesus replies: " 'You shall not kill; you shall not commit adultery; you shall not steal; you shall not bear false witness; honor your father and your mother'; and 'you shall love your neighbor as yourself.' "

In his discussion of this passage in his encyclical *Veritatis Splendor,* Pope John Paul II points out that Jesus is not saying that these commandments are the only ones you must keep. He picks out some important ones as a way of telling the young man that he must keep the whole law — the whole teaching of Moses. Indeed, by implication, Jesus is telling the man to observe the Beatitudes, the Sermon on the Mount, and all of His teaching, which is set forth for us in the New Testament.

Here is our first principle of discerning a life vocation. The foundation of any vocation is a general call to holiness and knowledge of God. We are all after eternal life — that which lasts. We are pursuing that which continues to exist when everything else blows away. To achieve this, Jesus is saying, we need a relationship with God. We don't pursue eternal life. We pursue *He who is eternal*.

In His prayer to the Father at the Last Supper, Jesus says this plainly: "Now this is eternal life, that they should know you, the only true God, and the one whom you sent, Jesus Christ" (Jn 17:3).

The object of every vocation is God. It's not building a better society, renewing the Church, having a family, fulfilling yourself, helping people, or confronting new challenges. All these things may be involved in a vocation, but the primary objective — the goal of the priest or sister, husband and wife, single lay man or lay woman — is to love God.

We do this by establishing the foundations of the Christian life. These are the four sections of the Catholic catechism — the commandments, the creed, the sacraments, and prayer. Without these being alive in your life, without fidelity to the commandments and zeal for the faith, without a life as a Catholic and a Christian, you don't have the foundation for a specific vocation. The rich young man says to Jesus, "I want to be your special follower." Jesus replies, "Get your life in order first."

To put this in the terms of this book, the first step to discernment of a life vocation is *conformity* to God. We submit to His law and we submit personally to Him. He says, "Now this is eternal life, that they may know you the only true God and Jesus Christ whom you have sent" (Jn 17:3). Our conformity is an act of submission to a *Person* whom we know. Should we proceed into a life commitment without this foundation, we will need to lay this foundation later.

I can actually point to a moment when the pieces of my fragmented life came together for the first time. I was a sophomore at college, going in several directions at once, trying to keep my options open, plagued, in particular, with questions about God. On the day of my nineteenth birthday I went into the woods on the outskirts of town and grandly announced to God, "I'm staying here in the woods until you do it."

What was "it"? To let me know for sure that He existed. To reveal how I could know Him. To speak to me.

I stayed in the woods all day and into the evening. I was hungry and thirsty and it was getting cold. I was a little scared, but I was stubborn. I was determined to stay in the woods until I got an answer.

The answer came at around 8:30 in the evening. The puzzle of God suddenly cleared up in my mind. A conviction grew in me that He did indeed exist and that the Church was indeed an institution that told the truth about Him. I could have confidence in it. The Lord spoke to my heart too. He loved me. He would forgive my sins and heal my wounds. I was home. All this was a free gift of God. I was a desperate case, so he had pity on me and gave me everything at once.

This was the foundation. The vocation I discerned later flowed from this relationship with the Lord that began that evening in the woods. That was the key. That relationship has been there ever since.

The rich young man says, "I have observed all the commandments. What do I still lack?"

The first stage of discernment is establishing a relationship with God. The second stage is listening to Him. We detect His Spirit moving in our spirits. We hear what He is saying to us. We strain to detect that specific call within the general call to know, love, and serve God. Scripture says of Mary that "she treasured all these things in her heart" (Lk 2:19). Another translation says that she "pondered" them; another that she "kept" them in her heart. We are called to do the same, to listen deeply, thoroughly, until we get it.

The key to testing the specific vocational call is the test of *conversion*. Our response to the vocation involves converting our life more deeply and fully to the Lord. The call to religious life means a special call of service and self-surrender. The call to marriage always means a conversion from a self-centered life to a life centered on a spouse and children. Being "in love" is important but not sufficient. Marriage, as well as the religious vocation, involves a commitment to the loving service of others.

Life vocations also involve *consistency* among the call, the person called, and the spouse. In the marriage vocation, the spouse is the prospective partner. In the religious vocation, the spouse is the Church.

For women religious, the spouse is Christ, based on the understanding that their union with the Church, which is the spouse of Christ, makes them individually the spouse of Christ in a special way through their vows. Male religious could say the same, of course, but it is more meaningful for them to see the Church as feminine and therefore the spouse they embrace when they make their vows.

Sometimes we know we are called to marriage or the religious life long before we find someone we would like to marry or a religious order we would like to enter. Sometimes we understand our vocational call only when we meet the people we would like to spend our life with. In any case, the call will be consistent with what has gone on before in our lives.

The consistency of the vocation will be tested over a period of time. A couple will go through years of acquaintance and courtship to discern the vocation. People discerning religious vocations will spend years in seminary and formation before making vows for life. We say that married people are "made for each other." We say that priests and nuns and brothers "have a vocation." What we are saying is that they pass the consistency test.

The same is true for vocations to the single life. Many people are called to actively embrace singleness in order to care for family members, join a lay apostolate, or other life of service. There must be consistency among the service, the person, and the call to singleness, just as there must be conformity to the gospel and an awareness of how the call will lead to a greater conversion of one's life.

As you discern a life vocation, it's important to *live* consistently. Start living now what you believe is your vocation. Eliminate the contradictions. As a decision about marriage approaches, both partners would stop dating other people and devote their attention exclusively to each other. Men and women might date in the early stages of thinking about a religious vocation. As they move toward a decision, however, it's important to begin to live the celibate call, without romantic relationships.

I know how painful this can be. I was engaged to be married when I heard the Lord's question in my first year of law school: "Will you give me your whole life?" And I knew that by saying "yes" to him, I was saying "no" to my fiancee.

Pray for steadfastness and consistency. Develop what the scriptures call single-mindedness and single-heartedness as you pursue what God desires. Many people listen too long. Listening keeps the options open. You can get married or be a priest. You can make a lot of money, get a Ph.D., write the great American novel, be a movie star, be the quarterback for the Redskins. To pursue God's plan for you, you must close off options. Welcome this. Get rid of your riches, whatever they are, and get in line as a follower of Jesus.

When I began to hear God's specific call, I hedged a bit. It happened in my first year of law school at Harvard. I was walking back from Mass during Lent across the lawn at Longfellow's house, when the Lord stopped me in my tracks. How did I know it was the Lord? you ask. I *knew*. Nothing else could have stopped me. Then he asked a question: "Will you give me your whole life?"

I knew this was something more than a general call to love and serve God. It was a call to something I didn't know anything about. If I said "yes" He would take me somewhere I wouldn't have chosen to go on my own. So, like a good budding lawyer, I said "yes, but…." I said, "I'll give you my whole life, but first let me finish law school, pass the bar, satisfy the parents, take care of this business I was doing." Sometimes I wish I had been able to say "yes" without qualification: "Yes, Lord, anything you want. Just tell me and I'll do it." But I hedged. Conversion is a process. This call arrived at an earlier stage in the ongoing conversion of my life, and I responded as well as I was able.

For years, I pondered these words in my heart. I wrote down what I sensed God was telling me about His call. I recommend this practice highly. Write down the ways you are hearing God — things people say, passages you read in scripture, stories of the saints, senses in prayer. Sometimes God will fall silent in our relationship with Him. But most often He's speaking; we're missing what He is saying. It's a little like a brand new shortstop taking infield practice. He can handle the balls hit right at him pretty well, but he has trouble with those hit to the right and left. Like the shortstop, we have to learn to pick up the message — to anticipate it, to respond quickly to it.

We can pray Psalm 123:

> To you I raise my eyes,
>   to you enthroned in heaven.
> Yes, like the eyes of a servant
>   on the hand of his master,

Like the eyes of a maid
on the hand of her mistress,
So our eyes are on the LORD our God.

Ps 123:1-2

Like the psalmist, we wait attentively, our eyes fixed on the Lord, our ears attuned to His voice. This time of listening can take many years. The important thing is to keep at it.

There are three ways to listen: pray, pray, and pray. We can pray with people, with scriptures, with the liturgy, in song with our hands raised in the air. Be sure to take some time to simply listen to what God might have to say. Place yourself alone before the Blessed Sacrament and ask, "Lord, what do you want?"

The Lord answers the rich young man: "If you wish to be perfect, go, sell what you have and give to the poor, and you will have treasure in heaven. Then come, follow me."

A life vocation is a two-way street. It must pass the test of *confirmation* — most critically, the confirmation of the spouse. The marriage partners must agree to marry each other. The would-be priest, sister, or brother must receive an invitation from their spouse — the Church.

The lack of a confirming invitation can cause great anguish. Lovers say their hearts are broken when their love is not reciprocated and a proposal of marriage is turned down. The same thing happens to people who think they have a call to the religious life. The call to a religious vocation is mutual. Both the individual *and* the Church must hear it. Since the mutuality of a religious vocation is often less well understood than the mutuality of marriage, I would like to say a bit more about it.

Dealing with the Church can be difficult. Sometimes we don't like what we hear from the priest or sister or religious brother. The novice director or the head of the seminary can misunderstand, fail to connect. They can even give bad advice.

But the Church is the institution the Lord established to carry out His work — including the work of discerning vocations to the religious life. God became man. He entered into human life. He works through human beings and human institutions.

In my own life, I went through a long period of confusion and uncertainty before the Church and I heard God's call for me.

I had heard the Lord's question, "Will you give me your whole life?" in my first year of law school, and answered, in effect, "Yes, but check back with me when I'm finished with school." God did precisely that.

After graduating from law school, I entered the Air Force and took the New York State bar exam. One morning a friend of mine waved *The New York Times* at me and said, "Congratulations, Mike, you've passed the bar. It's right here in the paper." Sure enough, there was my name, published in tiny type in a list of people who were now admitted to the bar in the state of New York.

I went straight to my room and knelt by my bunk. I had played all my cards. "Yes, but ... " was now simply "Yes." I had only one question for God: "What?" I said. He answered: "Religious life and priesthood." He was calling me to a double vocation — priesthood within a religious order. That was all He said. The rest was up to me and the Church.

It was messy. Although I was born and raised a Catholic, I really knew very little about the Catholic Church. I had stopped going to Catholic schools after the eighth grade. I didn't know any priests well. I didn't know how the world's oldest organization operated. When I thought of religious orders, I thought automatically of the Jesuits. So I looked up the Jesuits in the Washington, D.C. phone book, wrote down the address, drove over, and rang the bell.

I took the direct approach. "I'm Lieutenant Scanlan," I told the person who answered the door. "God has called me to a religious vocation and I'm trying to figure out where. I thought I'd start with the Jesuits."

I ended up visiting Father Avery Dulles, then a newly-ordained priest who became one of the best theologians in the world. He showed me the huge library at the Jesuit seminary in Maryland and told me I could spend my life there. This didn't pass the consistency test. I could study well enough, but the academic life had never appealed to me. Father Dulles left me with some good advice: "The vocation is the restless spirit of God within you," he said. "You keep following it to the place it's at rest and poured out."

I followed the restless spirit to the Dominicans. I knocked on their door in Washington and met a porter who was thrilled to meet someone who was talking about a vocation. He told me there were books of direct divine revelation: the Holy Bible and the *Summa Theologica* by St. Thomas Aquinas. This didn't sit well with me; I knew the *Summa* couldn't be on a par with the scriptures, and, in fact, the Dominicans don't believe that either. I could have investigated the Dominicans more, but I decided to look elsewhere.

I started to study Latin. This wasn't something I enjoyed but in those days Latin was the language of the Church, and I knew I would have to learn it. My tutor told me about a group of Franciscans in the area and suggested I visit. I did.

I talked to a priest who had been born in Ireland and grew up in Brooklyn. He was almost impossible to understand. He spoke a thick Irish brogue with a Brooklyn accent and he barely moved his lips when he talked. Two years later he would be my novice master. This time, he sent me away from our first meeting with one piece of advice: read about St. Francis of Assisi.

Francis was a revelation. As I read about him I began to be strongly drawn to the Franciscan way of life. I have monumental vanity and pride; Francis exemplified the humility I craved. I was drawn to a community life of brotherhood; this was the Franciscan way.

None of this was easy. I conducted my search for a religious order in a seemingly haphazard fashion. Some of the people I met confused me and I am sure I confused some of them.

What Does *God* Want?

Normal rational human criteria said I probably didn't belong with the Franciscans, yet the restless Spirit of God led me there. As I pursued the Franciscan way, it became clearer and clearer that this was where I belonged.

In June, 1957, I got in my little car and visited two diocesan seminaries. The seminarians looked happy and the priests were welcoming, but neither place was the one. Then I went to the Franciscan seminary in Loretto, Pennsylvania. I experienced community life there and heard the call to poverty and everything within me said, "Yes!" The Spirit of God was at home. I knew this was the place where I could pour out my whole life.

The process of making a life commitment is easily described. It's messy and imperfect in reality. We are dealing with sinners, not angels. The man and woman at the altar are two imperfect people exchanging vows of love and faithfulness. Every religious community and diocese is populated by people marred by sin. Don't look for the perfect spouse or perfect community. Even if you found the perfect partner, the marriage wouldn't be perfect after you joined it.

You need patience. You don't make the rules and you are not in charge. Courtships can be lengthy. Religious vocations can take a long time to unfold. There can be false starts.

You will change.

Those who are too rigorous, legalistic, rigid, set on things being a certain way, will learn to adapt and be flexible.

Those who like things to be loose and informal, never settled, will learn the joys of discipline and structure.

Those who escape into the spiritual to avoid the natural and the physical will learn how to embrace the messiness of real life.

Those who are too cautious and careful will learn how to leap ahead with God's call.

Risk-takers who leap before they think will learn the skills of caution and reflective deliberation.

Your life vocation is a treasure buried in a field, the pearl of great price. The grace is in the calling. Pursue it at whatever the cost.

Chapter 9
Giving Guidance

All of us give advice — on the phone to family members, at lunch with friends, to colleagues in the office, to neighbors over the back fence. Sometimes our advice is sought; sometimes we offer it on our own initiative. Often it's timely and welcome; sometimes it's politely ignored; sometimes it's resented. This chapter is, primarily, my advice to advice-givers who are asked for their counsel. It can also be read as a "hands-on" overview of the discernment process in practice, of interest to all who are in the process of discerning a course of action. It should be especially useful for those who have responsibility for others or who are frequently sought out by others because of their age, maturity, or position. These guidance-givers include parents, pastors, counselors, spiritual directors, teachers — anyone who is often approached by others with the request: "I need to make an important decision. Can you help me sort it out?"

I have heard this request in various forms almost daily for many years, and I have tried to respond to it as often as I can. I hear it from the students who surround me at the university. I hear it from faculty, staff, and my brother friars. I am approached by people I have come to know in my travels and speaking. Here I want to distill some lessons from this experience for people who give guidance themselves.

I will outline a general approach I try to follow. This is not a checklist I run down with everyone who consults me. Every person and every situation is different. But these are the areas I try to touch upon and some of the difficulties in guidance that I frequently encounter.

*You **can** be at peace.* I try to assure people who bring a difficult decision to me that they will be able to know what God is calling them to do. They will know in their deepest being, in their heart of hearts, that something is right to do. Many people need this reassurance. They are not sure they will ever know God's will or, if they do, that this will necessarily bring them peace.

We begin in prayer. I quote two verses from the Psalms that are favorites of mine for these situations: "Take delight in the Lord and He will give you the desires of your heart" (Ps 37:4) and "I am your servant. Give me wisdom that I may know your decrees" (Ps 119:125). We pray the prayer to the Holy Spirit together: "Come, Holy Spirit, fill the hearts of your faithful…." We add other prayers appropriate to the situation. We ask the Holy Spirit to inspire us and lead us to true wisdom.

Use your mind. I advise the person that in the ordinary course of events they are to use their minds to reach conviction in their hearts. I read the beginning of Romans 12: "I urge you therefore, brothers, by the mercies of God, to offer your bodies as a living sacrifice, holy and pleasing to God, your spiritual worship. Do not conform yourselves to this age but be transformed by the renewal of your mind, that you may discern what is the will of God, what is good and pleasing and perfect" (Rom 12:1-2).

We talk about renewing the mind — centering the intellect and the will totally on God and what He wants for us. I like to quote scripture to reinforce this point, including the greatest commandment: "Love the Lord your God with your whole heart, your whole mind and with all your strength; and love your neighbor as yourself" (Mk 12:30-31). The purpose of our discussion, indeed, the purpose of our lives, is to seek out and live God's will for us.

What are the options? I ask the person what he or she thinks God wants them to do. If they present alternate possibilities, I ask which one they are inclined to think is God's will.

From students and younger people, the possibilities I hear most frequently are: Should I marry? Should I be a religious or a priest? Should I break up this relationship with the person I'm dating? Should I change my major course of study in school? Should I go to a certain graduate school? Should I spend my summer in volunteer missionary work or should I take a job at home? Should I room with these particular people? Should I direct my future career into work for the Church?

From recent graduates and older people I hear: Is God calling me to move and change my job? Should I go back to school? I thought I was called to marriage but it's been many years and I haven't found anyone to marry. Should we adopt children? Should I join a lay community or apostolate? How do I deal with my strong attraction to the married person at work who seems to be flirting with me?

If the person prefers one alternative from among the many possibilities, we discuss it and test it.

A couple of scripture passages I use to set the right tone for this discussion are: "Test everything, retain what is good (1 Thes 5:21) and "Discern what is of value so that you may be pure and blameless for the day of Christ" (Phil 1:10).

Does it conform to God's law? Most serious Catholics will readily submit to the commandments of God and the teachings of the Church. Indeed, the question is usually "What does *God* want?" Seldom will a proposed course of action be inconsistent with God's law.

However, a careful review of the priorities involved in the person's state of life will frequently cast a helpful new light on the proposed decision or change. Such statements as "I am first called to be a wife and mother" or "My first priority as a priest is to serve the people God has given me" will clarify the matter if a new direction threatens to undermine these commitments or make fulfilling them more difficult.

You can also review secondary commitments such as "God has called me to be a teacher" or "My main service to the Church is in the area of respect for life." Deeply-held commitments of this kind lay a foundation for future actions.

Will it assist conversion of heart? In applying the conversion test, you lead the person through his or her spiritual history of turning away from sin and growing in love of God. You both consider how the proposed action fits into this history. Will it bring the person closer to God and a life of virtue or will it lead him further away? Look at how it will change supportive relationships, whether it will increase occasions of sin, and whether it will be easier or more difficult to practice the disciplines of a spiritual life, such as regular prayer, Mass and sacraments, sharing faith with others, the availability of spiritual directors and models of holiness.

Sometimes the process of discernment will end here as the conversion test shows that a proposed decision will make it harder for the person to grow in holiness. After going through this review, people will say, "I can see now that the Lord doesn't want me to do this." (More often, however, this conclusion comes after the next test — consistency.) At the same time, a new direction that involves considerable additional responsibility should not be ruled out simply because it might raise new temptations and challenges. Perhaps meeting and overcoming new challenges is precisely what's needed for the next stage of the person's spiritual growth.

Is it consistent with the way God has dealt with me before? The discussion moves to the consistency test: How has God led the person to this point? The difference between the conversion and consistency tests is often blurred. In both, you are discerning a pattern of spiritual growth. Does the plan under consideration fit in? Can the person see his or her life leading to this point? Does the person have the time, energy, and resources to fulfill more demanding commitments?

The question of marriage. Students and younger people will often bring the question of marriage to you for discernment. Usually the person will already be in love with someone; the question posed to the guidance-giver is: Should I marry this person?

The problem with this is obvious. A young person in a serious romantic relationship with someone is not in the best position to objectively discern whether he or she has the call, the character, and the maturity to assume the responsibilities of husband or wife, mother or father. The Catholic Church has developed many materials for pre-marital instruction that go into these questions in depth. Unfortunately, most couples begin to deal with them only after they become engaged and set a wedding date.

If you give guidance to young people, you will frequently encounter difficulties caused by the characteristically different ways men and women view the question of commitment. Often, the man will be sure about having fallen in love, but will put off to the very end the question of whether he is ready or inclined to assume the responsibilities of marriage. Many a woman has been shocked to discover that her man is not necessarily proposing marriage when he declares his love for her and says he wants to be with her always.

A man and woman in a serious relationship should begin to deal with the vocation of marriage at as early a stage as possible, before the emotional temperature rises and commitments are made. They should discuss the question with those who can help them and make use of pre-marriage courses, Engaged Encounter, counseling, and personality testing.

What, if anything, confirms the wisdom of the proposed action? Usually the individual will tell you several ways that his or her course of action appears to be confirmed. Friends will endorse it. Circumstances will change in surprising ways to make the act possible. They may have detected special spiritual signs that seem to affirm it.

In large decisions — marriage, religious vocation — the confirmation of another party is required. Two parties, not one, make marriage vows. The Church as well as the individual assent to a call to a religious vocation.

You will often encounter knotty problems in this discussion of confirmation. What does it mean when the signs are negative while the disposition of the person's heart is positive? Parents and family are opposed, circumstances seem to block action, but the person still thinks the proposed course is the right one. Is this a question of timing, should the whole matter be reexamined, or should the signs be disregarded?

What is the relative importance of confirming signs — or the lack of them? How important is the approval of others? What does it mean when it looks very easy, or very difficult, to implement the decision?

Be careful not to let the discussion of these complexities overwhelm the discernment process. Difficulties tend to become more complex the longer they are discussed. Move expeditiously to the final test — conviction of the heart. This is the decisive test.

In my experience, it is often helpful to write down the most important items of confirmation — or the lack of it. In fact, it is usually a good idea to summarize the conclusions you reach at each stage of this review for later prayerful consideration.

Interpreting spiritual signs. Signs have their place. Signs appear frequently in scripture. "And this will be a sign for you: you will find an infant wrapped in swaddling clothes and lying in a manger," the angel told the shepherds (Lk 2:12). Gideon repeatedly prayed for signs that God wanted him to lead his small force against a greater army. Jesus' miracles were signs of the coming of the Kingdom. At the same time, St. Paul explicitly warns against relying on signs rather than on the faith we have received (1 Cor 1:22).

In my experience, a person's account of spiritual signs is more useful as confirmation of the desire in the person's heart than as a confirming sign in itself. Often, the individual is fully convinced that he or she should go ahead; the spiritual signs are incidental or ambiguous points of confirmation.

What does your heart say? The test of conviction is the decisive test. What does the person sense about the moral certainty of the rightness of the call?

Engage the person in a discussion of their deepest values and desires. Ask a question like this one: "Putting aside all other considerations, including difficulties in implementation and other complexities, do you believe that this is the right thing to do?"

Or ask: "When you prayerfully think about going ahead with this, do you experience a deep 'yes,' a release and a pouring out, or do you experience hesitation and deep uncertainty?"

The standard of moral certainty is high in life commitments such as marriage and religious vocation, where the commitment is for life and time is not a great factor. The standard of the conviction of rightness is lower in matters where the individual has to choose the best of several alternatives in a certain period of time. In these cases, moral certainty is a practical conclusion that this is the right course of action as far as I can see at this point as a Christian in submission to the Lord.

An even lower standard applies in minor decisions that have a small impact on the person's life or the life of others. You can act with the simple conviction that this seems like a good thing to do, or this is what I prefer to do.

Help the person understand the various standards of conviction that apply in different types of decisions. Someone contemplating marriage should have a deep peace about such a decision and a powerful conviction of its rightness at this time to this person. But such a sense of moral rightness is not necessary, or even desirable, in a decision about which used car to buy.

Pray, pray, pray. The key to obtaining conviction is prayer. The Lord Himself — through the action and presence of the Holy Spirit — is the source of true conviction. We all need to pray daily for God to lead us in obedience and faithfulness.

I pray three prayers of consecration each morning to seek this conviction in my decisions coming that day. The first is the Prayer before the Crucifix, which I learned in elementary school. The second is the Consecration to Jesus through the Immaculate Heart of Mary, according to St. Louis de Montfort. For the third I alternate between the Morning Offering and the renewal of my Franciscan vows of poverty, chastity and obedience. You will find these prayers in "Appendix 1: Praying for Guidance," page 113.

I then bring the decisions and actions that I know I need to make that day to the Lord. I ask Him to give me wisdom and insight into his will and courage to pursue it. I ask the Lord for revelation about my decisions; then I wait and listen for a response. I test any response I sense according to the tests presented in this book — conformity, conversion, consistency, confirmation, and conviction. I then alternate between periods of listening and periods of prayer and praise until I am at peace before God with my approach to the decisions I will make that day.

The Spirit of God searches our hearts. He exposes our self-delusion and our basic propensity to sin. Often, when giving guidance to others, I read this passage from the Epistle of James and suggest that the person reflect on it:

> Who among you is wise and understanding? Let him show his works by a good life in the humility that comes from wisdom. But if you have bitter jealousy and selfish ambition in your hearts, do not boast and be false to the truth. Wisdom of this kind does not come down from above but is earthly, unspiritual, demonic. For where jealousy and selfish ambition exist, there is disorder and every foul practice. But the wisdom from above is first of all pure, then peaceable, gentle, compliant, full of mercy and good fruits, without inconstancy or insincerity. And the fruit of righteousness is sown in peace for those who cultivate peace (Jas 3:13-18).

What Does *God* Want?

The word of God pierces our motives and prejudices and cuts between "joints and marrow" (Heb 4:12). We need to pray to be purified this way, to be convicted of sin and to come to repentance. Much of the classical Catholic literature on discernment deals with the purification and growth in holiness that accompanies a sincere desire to follow God. One of my favorite passages is from Sermon V of St. Bernard of Clairvaux:

> The first stage of contemplation, my dear brothers, is constantly to consider what God wants, what is pleasing to Him, and what is acceptable in His eyes . . . . No longer do we consider what is the will of God for us, but rather what it is in itself. For our life is His will. Thus we are convinced that what is according to His will is in every way more advantageous and fitting for us. And so concerned as we are to preserve the eye of our soul, we should be equally concerned, insofar as we can, not to deviate from His will.

If we desire to pray this way, God will answer our prayer. He will give us the grace we need to pray as St. Bernard prayed.

I have included in the Appendix some helpful reference materials on prayer. I have also included in the Appendix an article I wrote for *New Covenant* magazine titled "How I Pray Now." Finally, I invite the reader to see my booklet on daily prayer *Appointment with God* (Franciscan University Press, 1987).

You will frequently encounter difficult situations where a clear answer is not forthcoming and progress seems elusive. See Chapter Six — "Handling Difficulties" — for more development of some of these issues. Here I want primarily to offer some Catholic principles of discernment that can be helpful in four very common situations.

Erratic emotions. The person's feelings about the proposed course of action are often changeable. When a burst of initial enthusiasm and affirmation gives way to uncertainty and unrest, no effort to move forward should be undertaken. It is standard Catholic teaching that enthusiasm and excitement can be produced by works of the flesh and even by the devil. Yet they cannot be sustained in the face of the gospel peace "which the world cannot give."

On the other hand, initial anxiety and reluctance that gives way to deep peace and quiet conviction is another matter. Ordinarily, the later peace and affirmation can be trusted.

Spiritual dryness. Many times, a person will experience dryness in prayer and even a sense of abandonment by God upon embarking on a new course that he or she was convinced was the correct one. This can be very disturbing, even causing the person to doubt whether the course was the one God wanted.

Aridity in prayer can be a sign of an advance or a setback in the spiritual life. Sometimes the discernment of an experienced spiritual director is required to sort out the spiritual situation. In any case, the individual should not presume that difficulties in prayer are a sign of God's displeasure. To the contrary, they are a common experience in a healthy spiritual life, and can be a sign of great growth in maturity.

What is authentic confirmation? Confirming signs are frequently contradictory. Care must be taken to put proper weight on each.

A common example is a serious decision — even a life commitment — that is endorsed by one's close friends and pastor but opposed by family. Searching questions must be asked. Are the family relationships healthy or tangled? Is the family in a position to know much more about the person's history and character than pastor and friends know? Do friends and pastor know the person well enough to be aware of tendencies to move impulsively or to grow quickly bored with mundane daily responsibilities?

These questions must be addressed carefully. At the same time, the individual must always remember that he or she acts out of his or her conviction, not someone else's.

A roadblock. All signs say go ahead, but one large obstacle prevents progress. The religious community or prospective spouse is reluctant. The loan is denied. The house does not sell.

It is a sound policy to counsel patience and respect for the time in which God decides to work. Important things happen while we are waiting. Other circumstances change. The enterprise is seen to indeed be shakier than previously imagined.

Very often, waiting is an invitation to go deeper with God. For those who desire to probe deeper into knowing God's will through growing closer to the mind and heart of God, I strongly recommend the twelve steps outlined in a wonderful book, *Divine Guidance*, by Susan Muto and Adrian van Kaam. I know and admire the authors and I have profited from reading the book.

Conclusion:
Go for Holiness

This book does not address everything that might be involved in decision-making. But throughout I have emphasized the one thing that is crucial in *all* decision-making: the continuing conversion of our lives to Christ. Our decisions need to bring us into an attitude of submission, obedience, and love of God. When we are uncertain about His will, part of the solution is invariably to grow deeper in our relationship with Him.

"Why did God make you?" asks the *Baltimore Catechism*. The answer I learned as a child is still with me: "God made me to know Him, to love Him and to serve Him in this life and to be happy forever with Him in the next." To desire this is to pursue ongoing conversion of our hearts.

I tell students at Franciscan University that a simple decision from the heart can change everything they do and experience in life. This decision can be summed up in three words: *go for holiness*. If this is the passion that drives us, the priority that orders everything else, all the failures and trials, all the opportunities and risks in our lives can be transformed. They can be seen as ways to grow in holiness.

Failure is an opportunity to grow in humility.

Frustration is a way to grow in patience.

Suffering links us to the suffering of our Savior, who suffered and died for us.

The needs of others are opportunities to grow in charity.

To *go for holiness* means to live wholly for God. It means to strive to "love the Lord your God with your whole heart, your whole mind and with all your strength and to love your neighbor as yourself" (Mk 12:29-31).

God wants us to embrace the truth that all the problems, difficulties, and disappointments we encounter are storms on the sea of life that are not meant to sink us but to sanctify us. Each storm is an opportunity to grow closer to God. As we grow closer to Him, we love Him more. As we love Him, the desire to serve Him grows. We hear Him more clearly. We make decisions more and more in accord with "His good, holy and pleasing will" (Rom 12:2).

Once again, I recommend *Divine Guidance* by Father Adrian van Kaam and Susan Muto as a fine book to assist further growth in Christian decision-making.

In conclusion, I offer these scripture passages, which have inspired me in desiring to know, love, and serve God.

> To you I raise my eyes,
>   to you enthroned in heaven.
> Yes, like the eyes of a servant
>   on the hand of his master,
> Like the eyes of a maid
>   on the hand of her mistress,
> So our eyes are on the LORD our God.
>
> Ps 123: 2-3

> Let us rid ourselves of every burden and sin that clings to us and persevere in running the race that lies before us while keeping our eyes fixed on Jesus, the leader and per-fecter of faith. For the sake of the joy that lay before him he endured the cross, despis-ing its shame, and has taken his seat at the right of the throne of God.
>
> Heb 12:1-2

Jesus endured the cross knowing the joy of perfect obedi-ence. We can know this joy too. Let us submit our hearts to the Lord and use our minds to "test and approve what the Lord's will is," so that we can enjoy His gift of peace in this life and His glorious rest in the next.

Praying for Guidance: Some Resources

Prayers of Consecration
Prayers I say in the morning before I place my decisions before God.

Morning Offering

O Jesus, through the Immaculate Heart of Mary, I offer you my prayers, works, joys, and sufferings of this day for all the intentions of your Sacred Heart, in union with the holy sacrifice of the Mass throughout the world, in thanksgiving for your favors, in reparation for my sins, for the intentions of all my relatives and friends, and in particular for the intentions of the Holy Father.

Prayer before a Crucifix

Look down upon me, good and gentle Jesus, while before your face I humbly kneel, and with burning soul pray and beseech you to fix deep in my heart lively sentiments of faith, hope and charity, true contrition for my sins, and a firm purpose of amendment while I contemplate with deep love and tender pity your five wounds, pondering over them within me, calling to mind the words which David, your prophet, said of you, my good Jesus: *"They have pierced my hands and my feet; they have numbered all my bones."*

Act of Consecration to the Immaculate Heart of Mary

(St. Louis de Montfort's Consecration)

I, [Name], a faithless sinner — renew and ratify today in thy hands, O Immaculate Mother, the vows of my Baptism; I renounce forever Satan, his pomps and works; and I give myself entirely to Jesus Christ, the Incarnate Wisdom, to carry my cross after Him all the days of my life, and to be more faithful to Him than I have ever been before.

In the presence of all the heavenly court I choose thee this day for my Mother and Mistress. I deliver and consecrate to thee, as thy slave, my body and soul, my goods both interior and exterior, and even the value of all my good actions, past, present, and future; leaving to thee the entire and full right of disposing of me, and all that belongs to me, without exception, according to thy good pleasure, for the greater glory of God, in time and eternity. Amen.

Renewal of Franciscan Vows

Since for the praise and glory of the Most Blessed Trinity, the Lord has given me this grace of living more perfectly and with firm will the Gospel of Jesus Christ, I, Brother Michael, vow to live in obedience, in poverty and in chastity according to the Rule and Life of the Brothers and Sisters of the Third Order Regular of Saint Francis confirmed by Pope John Paul II, and profess to faithfully observe this promise according to the General Constitutions of this Order.

Therefore, with all my heart, I give myself to this Brotherhood that, through the work of the Holy Spirit, the intercession of the Immaculate Virgin Mary, Our Father Francis and all the saints, I may fulfill my consecration to the service of God, the Church and all people.

How I Pray Now:
"Prayer Is the Most Important Thing I Do"
By Father Michael Scanlan, T.O.R.

From the November, 1995, issue of New Covenant. *Reprinted by permission of* New Covenant, *200 Noll Plaza, Huntington, IN 46750.*

The best way I can express how I pray today is to quote the Holy Father from *Crossing the Threshold of Hope*: "The pope prays as the Holy Spirit permits him to pray."

I find that the Holy Spirit opens and closes doors to prayer. It is the Holy Spirit who anoints in power certain directions in prayer, and it is the Holy Spirit who blocks other avenues. Though I must start prayer, prayer once started is not my own. As my prayer changes, so does my life. The Holy Spirit reshapes my life through prayer. I don't always cooperate, but when I do, I also see the results in a life change.

I am reminded of the refrain: "Melt me, mold me, fill me, use me." This is in line with the statement in the Catechism of the Catholic Church, "We pray the way we live and we live the way we pray." If we want to change the way we live, we change the way we pray. This is what the Holy Spirit does in us if we yield to Him.

A new sense of prayer comes from the experience of being baptized in the Holy Spirit, which initially leads to a new involvement in praise, an increased desire to pray and a willingness to pray in the Spirit rather than predominantly in mental prayer.

In my life, this new development meant an increase of prayers of praise followed by quiet prayer of rest in God's presence. It also meant dwelling more on the words of Scripture and yielding to the power of those words to touch my spirit and change me. In time, I saw an overall approach develop that became a pattern I could teach. I outlined this pattern (which was based on an analogy to a business meeting) and published it in the booklet "Appointment with God."

My prayer continued to change within this broad outline, as the Holy Spirit anointed some directions and closed off others with a sense of blockage or being walled off from the Lord. Frequently, the areas where I needed to repent, change direction, or give new commitments were the only ones with a sense of anointing or power. After I would respond, change would happen and then new areas would become anointed. Sometimes this process took many months before there was movement to a new area.

I experienced this process moving me to fervent consecration of life. For a few months, all the power in my prayer and the overwhelming time and effort in my prayer was concentrated on heartfelt consecration of my life. I used the Morning Offering, the De Montfort Consecration to Jesus through Mary, the Consecration to the Sacred Heart of Jesus, the daily renewal of my vows of poverty, chastity, and obedience, and other prayers of consecration and entrustment.

In a similar way, I experienced months of concentration on intercession where I prayed extensively in tongues after each petition. Some days I could pray for one hour using the petitions that were listed in the morning prayer of the Divine Office. There were other times when a simple quiet presence or regard toward the Lord would occupy me for an hour at a time. I also recall times when every line of Scripture seemed to come alive and grab my inner being.

It wasn't all action, however. There was a period of more than a year when dryness and desolation totally dominated. I experienced being broken and humbled before God much as a person would feel if left hanging from a tree, dangling while the elements of weather buffeted him. Prayer moved from an exciting encounter with the living, risen Lord to a reaching in the dark to a far distant and seemingly absent Lord.

While the manuals on the spiritual life deal with these various phenomena of prayer, it was the words of the Holy Father that gave me the best insights. In *Crossing the Threshold of Hope*, Pope John Paul gives the context of his own prayer in terms of Romans 8. Verses 18 to 31 are particularly relevant.

Verse 18 expresses the hope that should be in us despite present sufferings: "I consider that the sufferings of this present time are as nothing compared with the glory to be revealed for us." He particularly refers to the references on groaning. Verses 22 and 23 read, "We know that all creation is groaning in labor pains even until now; and not only that, but we ourselves, who have the firstfruits of the Spirit, we also groan within ourselves as we wait for adoption, the redemption of our bodies. For in hope we were saved."

Referring more directly to his personal prayer, the Pope directs the reader to verses 26 and 27: "In the same way, the Spirit too comes to the aid of our weakness; for we do not know how to pray as we ought, but the Spirit itself intercedes with inexpressible groanings. And the one who searches hearts knows what is the intention of the Spirit, because it intercedes for the holy ones according to God's will."

It is this mixture of sorrow around us and hope within us that leads to the groaning in the Spirit for the full redemption of our lives and our communities, indeed the whole world. The hope that keeps groaning and won't give up is the hope poured out in our heart through the Holy Spirit and the hope expressed in the last verses of Romans 8: "For I am convinced that neither death, nor life, nor angels, nor principalities, nor present things, nor future things, nor powers, nor height, nor depth, nor any other creature will be able to separate us from the love of God in Christ Jesus our Lord" (38-39).

I am certain that prayer is the most important activity in my life. I believe that whatever is worthwhile and lasting in my life's activity was first conceived in some way in prayer and then given existence in action. It is the necessary foundation of all my apostolic activity. I cannot love rightly, serve faithfully, or make decisions with wisdom unless these flow from prayer. For these reasons, I always use a journal, writing something from each prayer time. I always read the previous day's entry during the next day's prayer. I also make it a daily practice to pray over my schedule for that day. This enables me to come closer to God's perspective and His priorities regarding all that I will be facing that day.

There is so much more I could write. I pray daily the Prayer before the Crucifix, the Rosary, and the Divine Mercy chaplet. I open every meeting that I chair with the prayer Come, Holy Spirit. I believe that the Holy Spirit indeed comes and fills our hearts and enkindles the fire of His love when we invite Him into our lives and gatherings. I treasure the daily Mass, which I am privileged to celebrate, and the daily Divine Office. I find that the readings in this daily liturgy always have some special application for my life.

I thank God regularly for the baptism in the Spirit and I endeavor to use the charismatic gifts, particularly the gift of tongues, on a daily basis. I schedule myself to go to one special charismatic praise gathering each week. I was encouraged by my recent experience of being next to the Holy Father at his morning Mass, and as he stopped at the intervals for personal prayer in the Mass and groaned in the Spirit, I was able to join in the groaning with prayer in tongues and discover that our prayers were most compatible following the same rhythm.

This is how I pray today. It is God's gift operating as the Holy Spirit permits, and changing as God ordains in his merciful love.

Worksheets for
Decision-Making

In this book, I have often recommended writing down considerations and conclusions you reach as you work through a major decision. The worksheets on the following pages are a useful tool for reaching decisions. I list those headings and questions that are most helpful in coming to conclusions under each test. I also provide room for you to write your own conclusions and helpful notes.

Worksheet 1: Does It Conform to God's Will?

1. Relevant commandments of God

2. Relevant teachings of the Church

3. Existing commitments that bear on the decision (work, family, etc.)

4. Existing "calls" from God that might contradict the current proposal

5. Might the current proposal hinder a spirit of submission and obedience to God and His Church?

Conclusions about Conformity

Worksheet 2: Does It Encourage Conversion?

1. Will the proposed direction lead to a closer union with God?

2. Will the proposed direction lead to a more faithful discharge of my primary responsibilities?

3. Does the proposal involve an unnecessary occasion of sin?

4. Does the proposal foster a spirit that says, "Go for holiness"?

Conclusions about Conversion

Worksheet 3: Is It Consistent?

1. **WHAT?** Is it consistent with God's earlier calls in my life?

2. **HOW?** Is it consistent with how God has dealt with me in the past?

3. **WHO?** Is it consistent with whom God has used in the past to lead me to His will?

4. **WHEN?** Have I heard His call at the same time (or in the same way) that I have heard Him in the past? (Daily prayer time, after communion, on annual retreat, etc.)

5. **WHERE?** Have I heard His call in the same place or under the same circumstances that I have heard Him in the past? (In church, during a walk in the woods, in a special place of prayer, etc.)

6. **HOW MUCH?** Is the cost, including possible negative effects, consistent with my established priority of values?

Conclusions about Consistency

Worksheet 4: What Confirms It?

1. Is it confirmed by those who are involved in the proposal?

2. Is it confirmed by apparent miraculous or spiritual signs?

3. Is it confirmed by people who know me and are in a position to give godly direction to me?

4. Is it confirmed by circumstances -- either extraordinary or which make the direction possible?

5. Are there other signs that seem to confirm or deny the validity of the proposition as from God?

Conclusions about Confirmation

Worksheet 5: Does the Heart Say 'Yes'?

1. Do I have moral certainty about the proposal?

2. Can I say that I believe in my heart that this is the right thing to do?

3. Of my alternatives, of which I must choose one, is this the one I believe is right?

4. Am I convinced that this is simply a good thing to do without any appreciable negative consequences following?

5. Am I paralyzed with difficulties or uncertainties and therefore have to appeal to other principles or to guidance from others?

Conclusions about Conviction. Actions to be taken.

For Further Reading

I. For deepening an understanding of God's communications

Divine Guidance, Susan Muto and Adrian Van Kaam, Servant Books, Ann Arbor, MI, 1995.

Seeking Jesus in Contemplation and Discernment, Robert Faricy, Christian Classics, Westminster, MD, 1983.

Discernment: A Study in Ecstasy and Evil, Morton Kelsey, Paulist Press, New York, 1978.

Is Talking to God a Long Distance Call? How to Hear and Understand God's Voice, John J. Boucher, Servant Publications, Ann Arbor, MI, 1990.

The Place of Discernment, William Yeomans, The Way, London, 1989.

II. Ignatian Rules of Christian decision-making and discernment of spirits

These principles have been studied and incorporated at various points in the text. For a consistent Ignatian understanding refer to the following:

For Christian decision-making:

The Spiritual Exercises of St. Ignatius Loyola, Lewis Delmage, SJ, Joseph F. Wagners, Inc., Hawthorne, NY, 1968 (see paragraph #175, in particular).

For discernment of spirits:

A Commentary on St. Ignatius' Rules for the Discernment of Spirits, Jules J. Toner, Institute of Jesuit Sources, St. Louis, MO, 1982.

See also:

Weeds among the Wheat, Thomas H. Green, Ave Maria Press, Notre Dame, IN, 1984.

The Spiritual Life: A Treatise on Ascetical and Mystical Theology, Adolphe Tanquerry, Society of St. John the Evangelist, 1930.

III. For enriching an understanding of our responses to God

The Collected Works of St. John of the Cross, trans. Kieran Kavanaugh and Otilio Rodriguez, Institute of Carmelite Studies, Washington, DC, 1979.

Abandonment to Divine Providence, Jean-Pierre de Caussade, trans. John Beevers, Image Books, Garden City, NY 1975.

The Imitation of Christ, Thomas á Kempis, trans. William C. Creasy, Ave Maria Press, Notre Dame, IN, 1989.

Obedience, Raniero Cantalamessa, St. Paul Publications, Middlegreen Slough, England, 1986.

The Practice of the Presence of God, Brother Lawrence of the Resurrection, trans. John J. Delaney, Image Books, Garden City, NY, 1977.

Introduction to the Devout Life, St. Francis de Sales, trans. Allan Ross, London, Burns, Oates, and Washbourne, Ltd., 1924.

IV. For a deeper understanding of the teaching of Fr. Michael
Scanlan see his other books:

The Power in Penance, Ave Maria Press, Notre Dame, IN, 1972
(out of print)
Inner Healing, Paulist Press, Ramsey, NJ, 1974 (out of print)
And Their Eyes Were Opened, with Ann Thèrese Shields, Ser-
vant Books, Ann Arbor, MI, 1976 (out of print)
A Portion of My Spirit, Carillon Books, 1979 (out of print)
Deliverance from Evil Spirits, with Randall J. Cirner, Servant
Books, Ann Arbor, MI, 1980
The San Damiano Cross (booklet), Franciscan University Press,
Steubenville, OH, 1983
Prayers and Blessings for Daily Life in Christ (booklet), with
Fr. John Bertolucci, Franciscan University Press,
Steubenville, OH, 1983
Turn to the Lord — A Call to Repentance (booklet), Servant
Books, Ann Arbor, MI, 1984
Titles of Jesus (booklet), Franciscan University Press,
Steubenville, OH, 1985
Let the Fire Fall, Servant Books, Ann Arbor, MI, 1986
Healing Principles (booklet), Servant Books, Ann Arbor, MI,
1987
Appointment with God (booklet), Franciscan University Press,
Steubenville, OH, 1987
Repentance (Catholic Bible Study Guide), Servant Books, Ann
Arbor, MI, 1989
The Truth About Trouble, Servant Books, Ann Arbor, MI, 1989
Rosary Companion, Franciscan University Press, Steubenville,
OH, 1993